For Hannah

This is a very special book of poems written by

Regular Talk, Only Shorter

my sister (who was also a social worker).

I hope you enjoy it and I also hope you have a wonderful summer and next year-

My best,

Jane

REGULAR TALK, ONLY SHORTER

Poems

Diane Brauer

Library of Congress Number: 2003096109
ISBN : Hardcover 1-4134-2848-7
Softcover 1-4134-2847-9

This book was printed in the United States of America.

To order additional copies of this book, contact:
Xlibris Corporation
1-888-795-4274
www.Xlibris.com
Orders@Xlibris.com
20830

CONTENTS

Preface

by Jane Honoroff

This project of editing and sorting through my sister's life's work of poetry has been bittersweet. It has been a journey of love and joy and laughter, and it has been a reminder of loss and sadness and pain. There were many days in which I laughed out loud one minute and cried, large box of tissue in hand, the next. I kept wanting to call my sister to read to her one of the poems where she got it exactly right.

I know she would have loved this book. I know because she told me, before she died, that she wanted me to do this. "Not one of those xeroxed copies. I want it published, with binding."

So here it is, for you, Diane, with love.

What I'd really like

is to

gather some people

together

maybe fill

Soldiers' Field

in Summer

at dawn

& read them

every poem

I ever wrote

& they would stay

all day

& laugh & cry

& go home

sane

Acknowledgements

There is no way, absolutely no way, this book could have been completed without the loving, tender emotional support and patient, non-judgmental technical (computer) support of my husband, Brad. Our partnership in all things is the sustaining canvas of my life. Many thanks go to my dear friend, Ruth Whitney, who held my psychic pieces together when the going got rough and also helped edit the text. To Sara Brockway, who sorted through backs of shopping lists and some truly awful handwriting and even worse spelling to transfer this body of work into the necessary computer format, I am forever grateful. Thanks also to Bill Brauer who was the inspiration for a large number of poems and who had the difficult task of gathering all the original poems from their assorted piles and corners, as well as helping with general editing decisions, and to Isaac and Gretchen Flores who put on disc the family photos included in the book, and to Sloan Sable for sharing the wonderful cover photo taken on our trip together to China. Finally, to my sons Ben and Jake, and my daughter in law, Denise, whose very existence reminds me of the profound meaning of family legacy, for whom I daily give thanks for the joy and richness they bring to our lives.

J. H.

Self

Sure
I make fun
of vegetarians
anyone would

But still,
I would like to be
the kind of person who
chooses to eat fruit
of my own free will
& loves pasta
with steamed
vegetables,
instead of
Quarter Pounders
with cheese
& Dunkin Donuts,

But I'm not
that kind of person

I'm
the other
kind

GAMES

if all the

"I should haves"

and

"if onlys"

and

"what ifs"

disappeared

there would be

only me

I sometimes think
life is
very weird
&
I just don't get it
but
maybe there's nothing

to get

(or maybe there is,
& everyone gets it
but me)

or maybe I, alone,
get it

So
it's all about

letting go

of
just about
everything

OK . . .

but, can I keep that?
I'm very attached
to that

That goes too, hmmm

so,
now what?

oh,

that

goes

too

TURKEY

The turkey is gleaming

the pudding is steaming

the mothers are scheming

the whipped cream
is creaming

the teenagers
are dreaming

the babies
are screaming

the grandmas
are beaming

& I'm depressed

"Whatever"—
notice how everyone
says
blah, blah, blah,
whatever . . .

Well what I
wonder
is
What do they mean
by
whatever . . . ?

❋❋

ODE TO ERIK ERIKSON

We had sex
& I wrote poems

generativity
takes many forms

Integrity
vs.
despair

& won

❋❋

Gratification
isn't
getting everything

it's wanting
everything
you get

❈❈

O. K.

so it probably

is good

to have

the necessity

of business trips
forcing

elective surgery
on those
who prefer
attachments
of

epoxy coated

spider webs

❈❈

I feel a poem

or three
coming on

Recently I've suffered

from acute

prolific-ness

Hidden
in the
opulence
of quantity

there is
quality

if you

are willing
to
revise

❈ ❈

When you love someone

or
(should I say)
when I do
there's a pronounced
tendency

(compulsion)
to
cathect
(glom onto)

that person

& congeal
or meld
—instant egolessness
is the foolish
game
of children
we are all
only
alone
& sometimes
if we're lucky
we meet a friend
& wave
as we pass

❋ ❋

We stare across

the sea & hunger
for the land

We sit on the shore
& gaze at the lake

We love what we
are not

&, (if we are lucky)
what we are

❋ ❋

I personally

        know this woman
(my age—give or take
a little thinner—give or take)
who just won a Fulbright
to translate Haiku from
        Japanese to English
& write a book etc.
        with a forward by
                Alan Ginsburg
                or someone like that

Would I trade places
        with her?

                no
Do I envy
        & want to
                kill her?

        yes

I'm trying

to think
of things I like
about myself

one is:
I know all the words
to all the songs
ever written

I also applaud
my choice of books

& my breasts

& how I cook
& how I love
& writing poems
& dogs
& how I am
with you.

❋ ❋

FRANKIE

As legend has it

my first gig

        at 10 months old

involved my mother
        saying

"Frank Sinatra"
        & me screaming
"Frankie, ahhhh!" in an
        adorable high-pitched
                baby voice
        (I had not begun
                smoking pot at this point)

I used to have fantasies, when I was
13, that he was
performing in a small
        intimate night club
& saw me in the audience
& we fell in love
(things got less clear
at this point, i.e. I wasn't
sure what happened after
the show)
        & he sang
Every
        love song

& we had the world
    on a string
& he flew
me
    to the moon
&
    in the wee small hours
of the morning
        we
    took a chance
        on love

❋❋

I dropped

    an ash

not in

    my wine

        I hope

doesn't look like it

        can't really see

            oh well

❋❋

Choosing

on the basis
of what
would look good
on
your resume

or your permanent record card

or your FBI
file

or your gravestone

may be

missing the
point

AGAIN AND AGAIN

again and again
and even again
pausing only
in the temporary oasis
of afterward
where echoes quiver
between resurrections
that we call
desire*

*see also desperation

rage broiling
grease splatters
tears sizzle
hopes fizzle

gagging on
what might have been

vomiting illusions
puking arrogance

choking
on Karma
writing poems
to keep
from killing
screaming silently
until tears clog
airways
& breathing becomes
gasping agony
& rage
a cancer
consuming space

I really like

    laying on this

old futon bed

and touching

    my favorite
        person
        &
    my favorite dog
        at the same time

while being stoned

& watching

    "Casablanca"

I'm 57

        & don't
                believe
        in anything

                except   you
and   Casablanca

        the problem   you see
        must reside
        in me.
(always before, I could blame
        some asshole
                I was
                        in love with,
        or married to)

CHAINS

Sometimes I feel that I must be free
& break these chains that are binding me
chains that are invisible
yet stronger than steel
chains you can't see
& yet they are real
my forefathers broke chains
        of slavery
and yet I know that I
        am not free
people call me rotten names
stupid people
        ignorant people
                people no better than me
man is to be very bright
yet you never see two horses fight
'cause one is black
        & the other white
Yet somehow I hope someday
        to be free
& break these chains
        that are binding me

The bottom line

is—
put that
in there

ah . . .

sometimes
you get
it all

a place
for everything
& everything

in

its place

❋ ❋

Don't get me

wrong
There were
many invitations

but

instead

I chose to spend

the evening
in my own

company
Thank you very much
I had the best
time
Let's do it
again
soon
I'll call
(have your people call
my people)

❋❋

ALONE AND

alone
          and wrapped in flannel
an affectionate feather pillow
curls itself and settles
surrounded
          by hair and cheek.
and hanging from   a blue balloon
          just above
an old memory with a new ending
          rises
and tangles with strings
of stranger shadows
          that sway   and hide   and shriek
                    until
                              yellow streamers
                              cut through gray
                                        announcing

                                                  day

❋❋

I made
100 prize-winning Christmas
cookies
& ate
one and 1/2.
Why can't
        I do this
with booze,
& other
        substances
I abuse?
Just lucky & thin
I guess

❧ ❧

panic

is only

the waves

slapping

a sun white
beach

making a joyful
splash

an anxious
symphony

a sunburned
heart

❋ ❋

RISKS

There is something I want
If I get it
I will be happy
If I don't get it
I won't be happy

If I think I will get it
& I don't
I will be happy
thinking I will get it
even though I don't get it

If I think I won't get it
& I don't
I will not be happy
thinking I won't get it
even though I don't
so—I think that I will
think that I'll get it
& even if I don't,
I'll be happy
until I don't get it
which is more sensible
than not being happy
until I don't get it

I never told anyone
          that I play John Denver
& Neil Diamond tapes
in the car on the
way to work

that I keep reading
my favorite books over
& over & when I finish
one, I kiss it

I never told anyone—
        that "thirtysomething"
was one of my favorite
shows

that I reread mysteries

that I don't cut all
visible fat from meat
        but eat it, instead

that I'm really not 5"3"
        (almost, tho)

that I cry
        at Bell Telephone
                commercials
(He just called to say
"Mama, I love you")

that I let my dog
kiss me on the lips

I never told anyone
I pretend to be
        a big band singer
& use a pencil
for a microphone

I never told anyone
I thought Eddie Fisher
        was sexy
                when I was 12

If your mother

turned 80

today

You could
theoretically
be 40

But,
you're not,

You're 55
&
on deck

I've always

thought

of myself

as a fairly anxious

person

except

one time

as the tiger
chased me

off the mountain's edge

there was a strawberry
I plucked it into my mouth,
and I said,

"Yuahmm,
this is good"

I couldn't sleep

        so I ran through
                early days
                        of love
        & won a Pulitzer
                for my collected
                        poems
                99, 98, 97
        & the teacher
                read my paper
                        as an example
                for all
                        to strive for
                                96, 95, 94
                & I sang
                        with Frank Sinatra
                        93, 92, 91
        & you reared
                & snored
                        90, 89, 88
                                and . . .
        the birds chirped
                & dawn's
                        rosy fingers
        rubbed red eyes
                & coffee
                        woke me

What I think of Y2K
can be summed up in 2 words! Oy vay!

❋ ❋

Memorial Day
reminds me

of something

Now what was
that?

❋ ❋

One might say

that
lack of
progeny

was the cause
or,
at the very least,
that which is constantly
conjoined
with the other
or
whatever
But I do feel

Human children
might have
been
just the thing
to stem the tide
of wine
that washed over me
& cleansed me
& killed me.

❋ ❋

SHIT HAPPENS

I used to think—shit will never happen to me
& then, well how can I prevent
        shit from happening
                or protect myself
when it does?
        or turn it
                into fertilizer?
        or learn from it
                so it doesn't
                        happen again?
        or, if only I had . . .
        or   what if I . . .

But now
        I know

        Shit happens

I just pledged

120 dollars
to public TV
for which
I get
3 video tapes
of Frank Sinatra

(I can justify this:
1 copy for my sister
& 1 copy
for our almost 25th anniversary)
plus
Frank isn't well
& he & Ella
sing
"The Lady is a Tramp"
together,
plus,
We could win
a free trip
to Italy.
Supporting public
television is
so—
uplifting

Even before I was 2
The first thing that I knew
was—I want to be
        comfortable
(only, I said *comverble*
        whatever)

I soon realized that
        to be comfortable
meant
        I needed to control
the entire universe

I worked very hard
        to do so
& then one day
        I was forced to say

That I just couldn't do it
        anymore
OK   OK
I never did
        control the entire universe

At first I took this
as very bad news
        but slowly & quickly
                I
                        leaped into
impermanence
        & had to give up
        being comfortable
                for being

Summer

is
closing in

& I
am filling out

I do here
highly resolve
to diet
& exercise
& walk
& get tan
just this once
more

❋ ❋

I'm having

a midlife crisis

I never thought I would

(a midlife, I mean,
not a crisis)

❋ ❋

PERMANENCE

I've been trying

to think of

some things

that never change
&
I couldn't

come up with

a single one

as the Buddha said

"All things are impermanent"

as my grandmother said

"This too shall pass"

They both appeared to be
remarkably
cheerful & relaxed
about the whole thing

Just when I thought
things were
going pretty well

My self esteem
took a bad fall

& I broke my hip,
metaphorically speaking,

& yes,
there's some
discomfort

but less
than when
I was
young

❧❧

The illusion

of permanence

is a black cloud
that hovers
over others
& even me, sometimes

Though

I know

it's a crock

How will I go?
damned if I know

Something will happen
& that will be thatten

It's all very sweet to take vitamins
& give up fat—maybe you just
had a salad with low cal dressing
& feeling virtuous you saunter across the street
& an El falls on your head

A not very good

something
awaits you

There is no way
to extend your stay

So here you are

now what?
First—not much
Second—this is what you
have—dream on hold on
(same thing)
or
let it go
wherever
& be here
right now
invest in the only sure thing:
impermanence
& you will be rich
NOW

One reason why
I didn't drive
all those years

was
extreme fear
of merging

odd really,
when I've spent
much of
my life

trying to

I think when I realized
I couldn't merge
with a person
(no, not even you, Ma)

that I discovered
I could
in a car
on Lake Shore Drive

APPROVAL

You don't like my hair
&
You think I'm dumb
& a lousy poet
& stupid & ugly
&
I mean *you*
don't like me
very much

When you consider
an investment
cost & return
must be weighed
a conservative investment,
bonds for example
or AT & T,
You won't get much
but the risk is minimal
if you want to
take a chance
you could lose
everything
or
win beyond
your wildest
dreams
But probably

not all that much
will happen

either way

❀ ❀

CHICAGO AUGUST, 1968

Jowls leer
Bayonets near . . .
It was perfectly clear
And through the fearing
Blazed the clearing
So bright   it extinguished
The northern star
Which fell   bewildered
From its usual place
landing in mace
On Michigan Avenue,
And floors above   they see it
With their horrified heads
(Thus retaining their virginity
For the wedding night)
And floors below   we see it
With gas-filled eyes
And battered bodies
Moving in passionate sway
With the enemy
Bleeding   away
Our own
In the crowded rape
Of Chicago

BABIES

Never been there

Never done that

I bet I missed

as much

as if

I had been

there

& done that

instead of

this

When I can't

fall asleep

I think about
when we got together

The songs
& the smells & the softest rain

if that doesn't work

I do Broadway shows:

Guys & Dolls

Carousel
My Fair Lady

if that doesn't work
I write my acceptance
speech for when I get the
Pulitzer Prize for poetry
if all else fails
I count sheep
but backward
from 100
99
98
9-7

New Year's Day—
a new beginning

a chance to denounce
a lifetime of imperfections
and vow
to be everything I'm not
but I wish I were:
5 lbs. thinner
an ex-smoker
a person who eats fruit
& jogs to her health club
& lives within her budget
until January 3rd . . .
So, this year I thought
I'd try something
the Buddha suggested
He said "Change your attitude
& relax, as it is.

(That may be harder
than giving up
smoking, even.)

❋❋

MYSTERY

Why is it that

I'm always

6 lbs.

away from

being

totally

perfect

no matter

how much

I weigh?

& why is it
that I never seem
to be able to
lose those
6 lbs?

❋ ❋

I'm a Midwesterner

now
I say good morning
to everyone
whether I know them
or not

I used to be a
New Yorker
& never said
good morning
to anyone

Whether I
knew them
or not

❦ ❦

Falling

into
the adult world
with little warning
& even less preparation

I was astonished

to find

there were things
I believed in

& even would (reluctantly)

fight for
"never sell out"
we said,
in the

sixties
&, as I near my own,
I'm proud
to say
I almost never did

❈ ❈

Some of the

        parts
hold up

longer than others

        like a car
each situation
        is idiosyncratic

in my case
        the
        cervical
vertebrae
        are disintegrating

        the colon
is exhausted
        & the teeth—
        don't ask!

But
the breasts
are looking good
yes, they've fallen
But they started
out
        by poking thru
my collar bones
so even gravity
has yet to leave
its indelible
        mark
plus
legs,
        eyes, knees
                arms

twat &
ass
all lookin' good
at 54
& the wisdom
of experience
makes up
for any number
of years
of youth
i.e.,
I'm hotter now
than I was
at 22
When I wondered
what you were
supposed to say
to your husband
while you were
having sexual
intercourse
I thought,
"How was your
day, dear?"
seemed loving
&
without appearing
overly
inquisitive

I didn't know
about
the part
where we scream
& come
& oh, God . . .
now,
I do

& I like it too
a lot more
than hearing
how your day was

❋ ❋

NO ONE'S PERFECT

I've done my best
at
work
& love

Freud,
I think,
would be satisfied

But I
was not

& decided to
be
a Bodhisattva

but all the while
I've neglected
my gums
dental floss
never meant much
to me

& now
my teeth
are falling out

❋ ❋

I'm waiting

for an

invitation

to greatness

Knock, knock
who's there?

"No No

it's us,"

said my fists

us?

yeah

ready or not

here
we
come

❋ ❋

SACRAMENT

DO YOU TAKE THIS WOMAN
    child of twenty-two
    who has not yet grown
    who cannot be alone

TO BE YOUR WIFE
    veil concealing need
    no breast could feed

TO LOVE AND CHERISH
    fetus yet to be
    umbilically tied
    to another baby bride

IN SICKNESS AND IN HEALTH
    embryo in white
    blushing parasite

'TIL DEATH DO YOU PART?

I came alone—

arriving
with myself

& discovered

it was
the wildest

mildest
party—

a coming out party

Spending the

evening in the

excellent company

of myself

I can't complain

Timid as a

baby bird
hiding under
stammers
&
details
the cowardly lion
stooped
with
shopping bags
of guilt

come on

put your toe in

jump

the water's fine

& so

are you

I know the words

to all the songs

& all the meals

that everyone

ever ate.

—What I don't know

is everything else,

in particular—

tomorrow.

My sister

who does not
fancy herself
a poet
said:
I will not be
a hostage
to panic

I
(who do)
said:
Damn
that's a great
poem
wish I'd said that
but I didn't

still
I know
the county jail
of guilt

the POW
of superego-ness
the cleaver
of cowardice
& courage

dead hope
awaits
freeze-dried answers—
reproduction rabbit-style:

makes pink bunnies
that breathe despair
and call it air.

❃ ❃

PROJECTED CONCLUSION? FUSION!

I hear
they've built
an atomic reactor
how superfluous
I've been one for years
am now working
to set the atom free
and put it in a bomb
and call it me.

❃ ❃

I've just read
all the poems
that ever
wrote me
quite a few

it surprised me
(some disguised me)
But more
exposed
a small pile
of truth
& I feel
about as
satisfied
as an old
fat
cat
who hasn't been
outside
very much
& has
a lot to learn

THE END

it's bad enough so
        but there is always yet
the inescapable penultimate:

                corpse scraping

        and so
                we go
        courteously repossessing
                a book
                        a record
                before
                        the exhausted coffin
                is lowered again

❦ ❦

all my poems

are stuffed
in a torn
manila
envelope
I'm tired
of being
my own
understudy
so
I rode a
motorcycle
into fearlessness

& made an
appointment
with my
internist

I made my

          thighs
what they are
          today
thru sheer force
          of will
& ankle weights

          they're not perfect
                    (too short—
          can't do much about that)
                    But they're
                              as good
as they can possibly   Be

I'm a constipated poet

          a Jewish Zen Buddhist

          a middle class lass

a flannel nightgown nudist

          but I'm *TRYING.*

I haven't gone out to lunch

in 2 years
I don't have time to get my
(seriously terminal)
gums cleaned
OK
that may be a
rationalization, avoidance
resistance
But
I also don't have time
to go shopping
or take my dog to the vet
or read
or, pee
or drink

❋ ❋

PLATO

chairness comes
before the chair.
careness first
and then i care
if i can dream to
i can begin to seem to
i dream
therefore
i am

❋ ❋

OPENING

Opening
    like an oyster
or a sloppy jar
        of honey
    or a window painted shut
opening
    like a can of coffee
with a mangled tin strip
    or a yawn

opening
    like a bottle of
        kid-proof aspirin
            (god damn this thing)

opening
    like a cunt
        atomic shrapnel
leaving a neat pile
of suffering ashes
    echoing mirrors
        of laughter

opening
    like a rosebud
just often enough
to believe
    it could be simple

Be Bold

in Boulder

Be chic
in
Chicago

Be Boss
in Boston

be New
in
New York

and make it there
and make it

everywhere
it's up to you

❦ ❦

I began meditating

because

I KNEW

enlightenment

was within my grasp.

but somehow

it just keeps

slipping thru my fingers

like frozen slime

am I doing it wrong?

I suppose

I'd even
complain
about
enlightenment

(It's so nice
here

they say
we're welcome
& yet . . .)
I always feel
I've
intruded
on someone
else's
coming out
party
someone named
Buffy
who plays tennis
& never heard
of
Dr. Atkins

Jews don't drink

        & so

        I must

be a wine spritzer

more cautious

        than
your
        average
Christian
        alcoholic
seeing pink
        Manischevitz
                elephants
        falling
                on
        deviated
                septums

during my twenties

Being thin

occupied

my energies

my thirties
were filled

with attempts

(unsuccessful)

to be fat

with child

Now I'm forty (one)

pursuing
doctorates
& condos

I'm losing weight
which is great

or would
have been
During my twenties

So far

Whenever
opportunity

has knocked

I've contrived
to be
away from my desk
for a
moment

can she return
your call?

alas
not

❋ ❋

I carry more books
in my purse
than Valium

& books
are a lot

heavier

❋ ❋

DICTIONARIES AND DREAMS

it's really
much too soon
to poke the dream
with words
          better now
to stroke it
with mute air
as it spins
on the potter's wheel.
only when it's done
need we name it one
time enough
when it's all thru
to label file and
Shrink it True

❧❧

having lived
          in mostly margins
I pre-expected
          limbo panic
          a half-familiar step to climb
                    But . . .
Panic is something
                    you can't pack for

❧❧

When I was born

I was given
a blanket wrapping
& a name
        people shouldn't put
                fireflies
                        into jars

❋❋

ART

Shame is an
        unpleasant emotion

worse than guilt

(although I feel guilty,
        saying that)

But the truth is
my visual
        perception
is not what it should be
given the activity
in general of my
        cultural attributes
I think I really like
        Monet, though
although so does everyone else
        in the world

Pretty safe bet
        even for the
artistically challenged

❋❋

Nothing goes

        to waste
in my house

except maybe

on occasion
        me

❋❋

I want a
        Burled Walnut
                Dashboard
& crushed leather seats
        in my red Saab convertible

                or not

❋❋

Instant gratification
        takes too long

❋❋

What is

        surreal, really?

❋❋

MEMORIES OF CHILDHOOD

You know how the odor
of burning leaves
brings you back
to being
5 years old
in the country
& you *are*

I remember giving the
big kids my candy
so they would let me
play with them

I remember corn on the cob
& toasted marshmallows
& poison ivy
& watermelon drippings

I remember a framed picture
of a soldier
who everyone said
was my father

I remember people cheering
& dancing

Because the war
was over

It's

so indulgent
to note

(serenity now)

What makes a person think

that being
vulnerable
is so appealing?

It isn't

Sometimes
        when I'm stoned

I see things

        so much clearer

                so, why?
                        So, what?

                so,
        I don't get it.

Maybe if you get
                too complacent

That's not
        so good,

& you need to
        relearn
                the lesson

That you don't know
                shit
        about anything

Whew—
        what a relief

QUITTING

It's time again to try to end
My relationship with my best friend
I love you more than anything
But lung cancer I fear you'll bring
and emphysema, that's there too
So it's time to part for me & you

I was twelve when we first met
& through my life, you've helped me get
All these years, just we two
How can I say "goodbye" to you?

But when they say my time is done
I'll light you up & we'll be as one
and I'll be happy once again
But in the meantime—from now 'til then . . .

A second, an hour—
            I'd best invoke a higher power
and patches & pills—whatever it will take
a former smoker of me to make

And when I've done four score & ten
I sure do hope you can smoke in Heaven
If not, I'll have to say, "Oh, well"
'Cause I am sure you can smoke in Hell
                        Hey Lucifer, got a match?

I used to be a bus person
head down
collar up

patient as a cow
clutching a thick book
Hoping for a seat

Now
scarf flying

I race down
El stairs
to
leap into the
bellowing caverns
& hop the clamoring
train then
lean casually
against the door
& stare ahead
neither avoiding
nor meeting
other eyes
bored & slightly
superior

I like to travel

But I like it

Best

at home

I guess that means

I'm an agoraphobic

or

a happy person

Probably

Both

❋❋

Food is no longer
a problem

I solved it
by becoming

an alcoholic

Now my body is thin

(only my liver
is fat)

❋❋

One of the best things
about being
Jewish
is

There are no
Jewish
alcoholics
so you can
drink
as much
as
you like
& never
have to
worry

❀ ❀

It was only when

I was no longer
afraid of the dark
that I discovered
there wasn't any

❀ ❀

It's not that I'm

any less
neurotic
I just mind
it
more

it keeps getting
in the way
like an in-law
or a tall person
who sits in front of you
at the movies

or a mosquito

❋❋

I'd like to be

        more
                autonomous

(& taller
        & thinner)

I'd like to be
        less scared
        & neurotic

I'll always
        wish
I was something
                more
        & something less
                I guess

But this
        is more
than OK
&   OK was better
        than
                I ever
                        hoped for

The lake is getting older
Have you noticed?
Certain rocks
taking new definition
eroding
or exploding,
in a way
(a very slow way)

I look about the same
but the mirror
has these tiny cracks
around my eyes

Despair
is there
Integrity includes it
excludes it
eats it for lunch

❈ ❈

I always think
of myself
as a very
anxious
person
(Ms. Oy)

But when I
remember
my several
marriages, mixed
race liaisons
experiments with
& addiction to
drugs
& making out
with Italian
boys I didn't
even
know
at the movies
in Mineola
when I was
13
then, I think,
"Am I the
first
psychopathic
Jewish
person
in history?"
& then I think
Nah

❋ ❋

There's nothing
quite like
getting it

There's nothing
quite like
letting go

coemergent
wisdom

❋ ❋

Sometimes

after a
hard day

I like to come home

& watch reruns

or reread
my favorite books

It's comforting
to know
what will happen
before it does

after spending the day
not knowing
what will happen
next

or what
is happening now

❦❦

I followed

my twat
& look
what

I got!

❦❦

cut thru it all

& find

a friend—

the best

myself

How ya doin'?
long time no see
Too long

sarcasm

is the Halloween costume

of sentimentality

cynicism
a patchwork quilt

under which Romeo sings
& does a few other things

to Juliet
such coverings

are opaque

& X-rated

& silly

can't even fool
an atheist
like me

Being

whatever
        the situation requires

        is taxing
                at times

—By Friday night

I just want
        to be me

—Someday
        I hope to

                know

        they're Both
                the same

❋ ❋

ODE TO OBSESSIONS

sometimes
when all the ashtrays
have been emptied
& all the mysteries
have been read

& all the ulcers
rinsed
with milk
or alcohol,
& all the shops have been lifted,
then sometimes
I get
to feeling a hunger
bigger than hope
& the feeling
that there isn't enough
food in the whole world
or even
in your cupped hand

& it's not a nice way to feel
& that's why
I'm glad
there are ashtrays
to empty
(& shops to lift,
& cars to hot wire)

the thing I hate most

is
I'm cute
(even when push
comes to
shove)

I try to be assertive
& rebellious
& have a career
but the truth is
despite all this
I'm cute

I try to be
lean
& mean
& keen
& clean
& I am
but also
I'm cute

SUBLIMATION

smear words
write poems

eat cock
care for a banana?

change

when it happens

is like a small

          earthquake

a whispered rumble

          announcing

                    a small shift

                    of ground

and a settling in

          for the moment

❋ ❋

THE GIFT

When I was three
I decided to give
my first gift
everyone left cookies
& milk for Santa
but I worried that
the reindeer would be
hungry flying around
all night
so I left them
a big bowl of oats.

The next morning
the oats were gone!

"See," I said to my friend's
older sister, a rather
cynical child,
"This proves there's a
Santa
or else
the oats would still
be there."

But

        suppose
        plucking
        the strawberry
        isn't the answer,
                either?
        It makes
                a good
                        story,
        but so did Noah
                & the ark
But
        just suppose
        (I'm just saying)
        suppose,
        no one knows
        the answer,
or,
        there is no answer,
just 'cause there's
        a question
doesn't necessarily
mean
there is an answer
my experience
        would indicate
there may not even be
        a question

You don't hear much
about
Otto Rank
in these days
of managed care

But separation anxiety,
& birth trauma,
I think he had
something there

Whenever I think
I'm ready to leave
There's always something
pulls at my sleeve
& whispers
"Stay,
I know
yesterday was bad
but tomorrow's
another day."

Once when I was five
I packed a peanut butter sandwich
in a red bandanna & tied it
to a stick
& ran away from home
for as long as it took
to eat it
& then,
I went home
to dinner
no one even knew
I was gone
even me, really
& that's how it's been
ever since

I get too homesick

separation anxiety
I guess you'd call it

can't seem
to ever get
away

not much else happening

I guess
I'll stay

The more

I know

how good
it is

The more

I disappear

& definitely

vice
versa

If only

I could be
stoned

all the time

I would be

a lot less

irritable

& if everyone

was stoned

all the time

we would never

have wars

But,
we can't

and why
is that
again?

I remember

in 1st grade
the teacher called
on me
& for the first time
I didn't know
the answer
so I said "Ow—my
leg hurts
maybe I have
polio"
and they called my mother who came
to pick me up
& for once
she wasn't too
worried
& didn't seem to
think
I had polio
which was a relief
to me because
by then I was
convinced I did

I drove downtown
        for the first time
                today   at 52 years old
& it went OK
        yes
I would have to say

        and then
                I drove home
& Ed was in the car
        (not driving, or so
        I thought, although . . .)
& moreover
        I merged
                my least favorite
part of driving
        with Ed shouting
instructions & slamming
on the non-existent
        brakes in front of him
It all worked out although
        I had the mother
        of panic attacks
But all that proves is what
a good driver I am
        hell, anyone can drive
when they're NOT having a
panic attack

ODE TO ODES AND ARTIFACTS AND LIKE THAT

the Greek's the thing
        forget the urn
does not an urn have eyes?
                                        hell no
        even Yeats
                always dreaming of Byzantium
which   of course
        he never   found
better far   to jump
or you'll never know
        the swimmer
        from the drowned

❋❋

There's humor

& all the rest
        is funny

❋❋

It's

        fuckin'
spring
        again
& some people
never learn

I can't believe
        I'm one
                of them

❋❋

Co-emergent wisdom
could be ambivalence
falling in love

Bill

The trouble with you is
we're sitting & talking &
suddenly
you get up &
go to another room.
Where are you going?
Why didn't you tell me
you had to
go to the bathroom?
What did you do in there?
Where are you going now?
Oh—the kitchen?
Are you hungry?
I guess
I'll just tag along.
What are you eating?
I'd like a taste, too.
No—not
that piece.
That one—the one in
your mouth.

So,

you're gonna
be
Diane Brauer
for the rest of your life.
Oh, the rest
of my life?
Yeah well
I guess so
sure
Why not?
It's the best
offer I've had

by a lot.

CHANCE

I know
one of us
is going to die
first
I just hope
it isn't
either of us.

first

we were
co-workers
& easily
became
good friends.
Then
I noticed
your hands
peeking
out of
your shirtsleeves
wondered
how your arms
might look
summer came
baring
short sleeve
shirts
and arms—
confused
I lowered my glance
to your pants
as it happened
and that
as they say
was that

When you're most comfortable
not having
a clue
to what it all means
What kind of a living
do you think
you'll make?

❋❋

I know I'm the
great love
of your life
But who
is
first runner up?

❋❋

I thought

I was
a terrier
until
I met
you
& calmed down
into
a golden
retriever
Now
I pant a lot
and can't help
jumping
when
you
come into
view

❋ ❋

first

they said
I had to have
my gums removed

then
I learned
I would work
the hardest
Bring in the most money

and make
the least

Not the best day
and you
cooked grilled stuffed trout
soft food
and massaged my back
(& my front)
& I feel
a lot
better

❋❋

Having my ears cocked
for derivative meanings
("cocked"—hmmm)
It's a great relief
to be with you
who
says what you mean
&
means
what you say

❈❈

COLORS

You never told me
that you
& your first wife
spent your first wedding night
in the honeymoon suite of the Newark Holiday Inn

A white 4-poster bed
reclining on a red
shag carpet
with pink cupids
on the wall
& heart shaped satin pillows

no wonder
it didn't
work out

❈❈

You used to never say
        what you thought
You were nicer then
        but this is
                a lot more fun

❈ ❈

I went a little

        nuts
                today
        But I kept
                Thinking
                when I get home
                        we'll have
                                champagne
& unplug the phones
        & you'll
                be there

& I made it home
                & we did
                & you were

❈ ❈

Tonight

we fucked

for

two hours

& now

you want to

talk 'til dawn

licks

morning

if there's anything

more

than this

I can't imagine

what

❋❋

Sometimes

foreplay

seems superfluous

You want it

straight up

It doesn't happen
all the time

but when it does

that's how
you
should
have it

Sometimes I was

a cheer leader
with a big bull horn
Sometimes an archeologist
searching for the
bones of truth
Often a lawyer
pressing an argument
or an existentialist
explorer of meaning
Mostly we sat there
saying nothing

I'd imagine
your
mouth
at my breast
suckling

Nothing really
worked
Did it?

first

        I had
                lobster

        next
                I'll have you

        It's hard
                to be depressed

        on nights
                like this

❈ ❈

It's time for you

        to be
the colors of
summer

                &

all the
seas
        soft winds
                &
        the coming
        everydays

❈ ❈

You are

the longest
homework assignment
I ever saw
close
&
deep

❦ ❦

School is good

for teaching
how tenacious
ego
really is

you are good
for the
opposite
reasons

❦ ❦

If it were

up to me

You'd be rich

Alas
it's not
But
it's up to you

❦ ❦

I confess

I've
cherished
your (sordid) affair
long past the
point
where the principals
yawning
can
barely (!)

crank up
a peck
on the air
to the right of
the cheek

❋❋

There may be

some nights
when you're home
&
I'm not
it's not
worse
it's just
the
reverse
& it may be
considerably
better

❋❋

When you're about to do something

that's very important
to you
(and you're the type of
person
who
prefers to be seen
sticking pins
into
Balloon Emperors)
its hard to know

how to act

not to mention

how to be

You know me

& you really
seem to like me

I wish I could say
the same
for myself

I almost can
thank you

What I've always
wanted to be
was
myself
(call me crazy, but)

You
have made that
possible

(even likely)

❈ ❈

I just figured it out
it's not that I
love more
or less
than you
we Just love
differently

My way
of showing love
is sticky
with cream cheese

Yours is salmon mousse
It seems to work
like caramel
custard
(I'm the caramel
you're the custard)

❈ ❈

You brought

champagne & lox

of your own free will

& I

was pleasant
(even charming)
about you're
impending trip

I wonder what

will happen

next?

❈ ❈

Sometimes I want

you
to do things
for me

that I could
probably
do
myself

When you do
I feel loved
(& dependent)

When you don't
I feel scared
(& autonomous)

❋❋

You're either

        in Tokyo

Singapore

        or Penang

I don't know which
        on a business trip
                for Motorola

& I'm a wreck
        I like to know
                where you are
That's why I get so
irritated when you
get up & leave the
room & don't even
say where you're going . . .
Now I don't even know
what country you're in
        How did people live
through
        World War Two?

Was it good for you?

It was good for me

&
if it was good
  for me
it must have
  been good
    for you.

❊ ❊

If you,

  who knows
    everything
      about me,

Thinks you need to
  “manage the news”

then I
  think,
    you must think,

I’m doing poorly—

  which makes me
    think so too

or why else
  would I need
    a Spin Doctor
      for a husband?

❊ ❊

You know that message
you left on the answering
machine from Penang?
Well, my plan is
to take that tape
& keep it forever
I guess this means
I haven't fully
accepted
the Truth of Impermanence

❋ ❋

Well there,

I wanted to
send you
off to Penang
with a lovely biscuit
& a big bang

& I did

Both were

Delicious

❋ ❋

I don't mind you
going away so much
if all the time
you were gone
could be
like the night before
you got back
or better yet
The actual night you got back

This is probably true
of a lot of other things
too.
Unfortunately I have a
strong tendency
toward the opposite
fairly common
among
our Jewish friends

❋ ❋

A strange gray

bird

with motor song

Takes you halfway
around the world

We wait here

in Illinois

❋ ❋

I was born too late

I understand
        boring from within

& protesting war

but I think the faxes
        aren't possible

& Internet . . . ?
        don't ask

❦ ❦

PENANG

You're going away

To a place

so far

That I don't even
know
where it is—
on the other side
of the world

& when you call me
it will be
yesterday here

old news

& if a dog gets
sick
I won't be able to tell you
until after (or before) the fact
I miss you &
you haven't even left yet
or you have
but not until tomorrow
my time

I

The plane
          from Tokyo:
You are back with us

II

Tomorrow morning is
the day I have been waiting for
          and vice versa

III

So   tell me all about Malaysia
& Motorola
          but first
tell me how much you missed me

IV

You were halfway across the world
& I was on my usual half
          in Evanston, Illinois
the whole experience
has left me anxious

I don't

believe
in much of
anything
but for 40 years
We've been
friends
I guess—I've loved
you—all that time
& now—
well—
shit!

❋ ❋

I must have

designed
your body—
how else
could
every shape
& line
& smell
be so
perfect?

❋ ❋

You remember me

before
everything fell

I remember you

when everything

was going well

or so we thought

we were
wrong

It's good
to
remember
how young

we were

It's good
to be getting older

friends are
good ones
a mirror

& old ones
        an old mirror

that embarrass
        you

with old truths
        &
make you smile

        with
                memories

❦ ❦

You are such

        a
                good Valentine
that you
        will even
                spend
my first
        non
                smoking
                        days

with me

(Either that
        or
you're
really crazy)

❦ ❦

Bonnie Raitt

really sings great

but all her stuff

sounds the same

you could probably
          say that
about every singer

          & everybody

                    as well
except for us

          of course

❋❋

THE FIRST

You were
the first really bridge
I ever dreamed:
          hands hugging
          sugarcone peaks
          slick with dripped
          vanilla snow

          feet tangled
          in ivy vines
          and picket signs

and we
          were something more
than time   and need
          something less than love.

Now
          the wrecking trucks rumble near
await my nod
                    which hesitates
          with something more than nostalgia
                    something almost   love

❋ ❋

When people

    plan & rehearse

what & when

    to say stuff

        to you

    it's engaging

    & humiliating

so don't do it

        anymore

THINGS I HAVE LOVED

Blue July skies

puppy kisses

old jeans
butter soft

August tomatoes

Amber mornings
lamb stew
& biscuits still warm

September roses

& you

❈ ❈

MAD AT YOU ON VALENTINE'S DAY

Instead of getting kissed

I end up getting pissed

A SOMEWHAT IRONIC TWIST,
ACTUALLY.

❈ ❈

It's almost

our anniversary

& we're having

a fight

or 3 fights

or 6

too many

to settle

before bed

You say:

no problem

they'll keep

I say:
(sigh)

I know

I used to think

        we had a
                perfect marriage

then you had
        an affair

now I know

        we'll stay
                married
                no matter what

        growing
                pains

❋ ❋

Come to

        find out
on our 10th
        anniversary
that your
        idea of me
is slightly
        off—
("my husband
doesn't understand
        me")
but then
        again
neither
        do I

❋ ❋

TENTH ANNIVERSARY

Where are
        the cakes?

There ought to be
        cakes
(though if there were
we probably
        couldn't
                eat them)
        still
Let there
        be
cakes

❧ ❧

Things as they are

        right now
mirror a
        single frightened
                figure
        frozen in the glass
        of a pond

so what do you do?
        reject things as they are?
                come on
        We both know better

❧ ❧

You—half empty

Me—half empty
stretching is painful
We gave in.
The illusion of completion
Binds us each:
You—half full
Me—half full

❋ ❋

I spent the day

studying structural elements

of family units

& patterns of interaction

& adult development

& homeostasis

while you

sat on a cushion

Then you came home

& we fucked

❋ ❋

People are saying

you had

an affair

even you

of course
I don't believe

a word of it

& the funny thing
is

I'm right

❀ ❀

I've repainted

your portrait
once again

muted more & less
than before

centered better now
more boldly
& subtly executed

not finished yet
or ever
I suspect
except in the
manner of
circle-ends

If you stay
            with someone
      for 10 years
            you learn a lot
some of which
      you never
            wanted
                  to know

      some of which
            you could never
                  have found out
            any other way

I wonder
      what eccentric

                  guest
      20 years
            will bring

Because of

what happened
my trust
is scarred

I know what happened
needed to
& was
my fault too

& given the choice
I'd rather be
realistic
than naïve

But still
sometimes
when you're away
I wish I was
stupid
again

You're the

you

of my
me

the object
of
myself

the self

of my other

the love
I'm in person
with

❋❋

WORK AND LOVE

I spent the day
writing about
drive derivatives
& libidinal energy
cathecting

I spent the
evening

doing it

❋❋

I'll never be

younger than
Springtime
again
&
usually that's just fine
But
there are moments
when it's not

& I remember
when just one look
or touch
could set us
off
into,
well,

Springtime

Today

I crept out
from under
all the footnotes

sniffed the air . . .
ah

sniffed you . . .
yumm

Took a short vacation
from significance

at the .05 level
& made a lamb stew.

(Does this look like the poem
of a person about to
drop out of graduate school?)

When I was little

        I didn't know
                much
about myself
                except
        that
                I loved dogs
& wanted to live with
        as many as possible

When I was 16
        I didn't know much
                except
I wanted to meet
        the love of my life
& live with him
        as much as possible

After several false starts

        I met you
                & we
                met the dogs (Sam & Sophie)
        & I got
                everything
        I ever wanted
                & I'm not even
                        that nice

❋❋

I could never

    tie my shoes
        'til I was 4
or even more
    & right & left? I was bereft
for jumping rope
    I had no hope

& Volleyball
    was worst
        of all

the only thing
    that I could do
was fall in love
    with you & you & you

a skill I practiced
        30 years
not without pain
    not without tears

    & then one day
I knew it was you
    & no one else
        would ever do
so I figured
    what the hell
I'll go for it
    I might as well

But you had doubts
    & all the rest
    which I dismissed
& flashed my breast

I had your attention

we both knew
and I capitalized
on the follow-through
we came together
in experience
& innocence
and keep on
falling
in love

❋❋

In a burst

of

Romantic zeal
&
admonitions
from the
friend
of the court

We got married
& have lived
happilyer ever after
than one might have

expected

❋❋

1st Husband

He took me
where

I already

was,
& really didn't
care for
all that much

2nd Husband

He took me
where I thought,
I ought,
to be
& I guess
so did he
strike 2

You & I
went somewhere
together

& still are

I'm not sure
where

But
I don't care
You're my favorite
person

of all the people
in the world

True,
I don't know
all the people
in the world

But you're running
a solid first
in my random
sample

❋ ❋

You are

closer than
a sunset
stronger than
a poem
sweeter than
a lilac

Taller than
the moon
Harder than
a star

❋ ❋

sometimes

        but not
                very often
you find
        the person   who
        could be
the love of your life
        & occasionally
He can only agree
& you know that
        You are very lucky
& this is very rare

That is the background

        When heaven
                        earth
                & man
        come
                together
& you think ah this is it
        I really have it this time
        until forever
Impermanence
        not my favorite noble truth
is conquered
        at last
the past
        with you

is as good as it ever
could have hoped to
        have gotten

The future
        can only be
        more & better
                than ever
& now, where we are
is the ocean
        crashing & slapping

a wake-up call

as each wave crashes
        the shore
with some fresh
        story that beckons
with new magic
        & pales in the
        green
                of your eyes

❋❋

You are

        about the
        nicest
boy I know
        or no, wait!
make that *person*
the nicest *person*
        I've ever met

❋❋

HANDS I HAVE KNOWN

One of the first things
I noticed
were your hands,
your fingers,
actually
they were so long

surgeon's hands
gynecologist's hands
& the nails
so clean & unbitten
Protestant hands
pianist's hands
artist's hands
lover's hands

I remember

the day
we met
you reminded me of
my puzzled
dog
Wolf
I remember
the day
2 years later
in Lincoln Park—
with rain
so light
we had to kiss.
"I love you," I said
"Damn," you said, "I wanted
to say it first."

THREE LITTLE WORDS

now
WHY
did I say that?
not even sure I like you yet
I guess it was
because it isn't true
& there's a draft
when we push back the covers

&
loneliness is lined
with fear
& because

sleeping buds
include
the someday truth
of bursting flowers.

I met my love
in a mental health clinic
(Don't worry,
we were staff)
That is,
we had degrees
& they didn't

Looking back
not only, did you remind me
of my puzzled dog Wolf

but also
of an incredible
Protestant God

The rest
as they say
is history

I'm having

myself

a merry little

Christmas
The tree

the fire
the dogs
the champagne

Joe Williams

& you

once

    when we were

staying in a chateau

    just
        outside
            of town
we decided to have
a picnic in the woods
    we went into the village
& bought a baguette
cheese, pate &
a bottle of wine
& pretended
    we were in
the French resistance
    you were Jacques de la Rouge
I was Danielle Blanc

pass the cheese, please

SUMMER

Summer is roses everywhere
    a sunny London dream
        Regents Park
        exploding roses
        dizzy with roses
        roses everywhere
        & you

BILL

Twenty-five years ago
you said "get your
toothbrush"

Who would have thought
25 years later
how beside the point
that would be now
(only in the concrete sense)

now
you would say
"Get your teeth"

or
that you
my love that I adore
would snore

pretty damn
good run
though

Timid

mountain climber
        wayward
                poet

        words present
boiling white rapids
                & you
are a canoe

THANKSGIVING

The first one

was an
afterthought

Crab meat, almonds

butter
& green onions
following an incredible
amount of sex

Then there was
the rear
of the duck
& the boots
& several traditional turkeys

intervening
But the best one

was pheasant
under you

sex

        with you
                is always
                        new
                & always

                        old
                traif
                        yet
                                safe

                impurity
                        &
                        security

                is the best fuck

FOR OVER AN EVER

for over an ever
        there was nothing:

who said   you
        could rumple
my neatly folded soul?

        oh?

                I did?

THE FIRST I LOVE YOU

the first
I love you

wasn't true
until
it spilled un-summoned
from first-spring lips:

an amazed puddle that hung
for a wisp of time
in air's outstretched hand
finally crashed,
echoing where it fell
like a pendulum
&
became true

after that
all I love you's were
subpoenaed
& meticulously poured:

no spills

or puddles

or springs

EXPLOSION

Remember

how it was

yesterday?

when we

were

a pair
of
heavy mirrors
hanging from
separate hooks
hating each the blank silver
glass
across the way
that gathered dust
and blocked the world

The Explosion
changed all that
the world splattered mud on silver

Today:
jagged glass
barely glued
on swaying wires

needing each
        the cracked silver
across the way
                to

play catch
        with
                the sun

❀❀

VACATION AT HOME

Let's do the grocery list
        & go out to dinner
                & fuck
        & take a boat ride

        & go to the art institute

                & a Cubs game
                        & Fuck
                & the beach

        & go to
                La Perequet
                        & fuck
                for lunch

and tomorrow

                if we live . . .

❀❀

10TH ANNIVERSARY POEM

I used to wonder
what people
meant
when they said

"I never seriously looked

at another man"

now

I know

❀ ❀

THE ONLY YOU

the only you
I knew
holds and molds
the you of now
in
knuckle-white fists
that strain
to keep the
handful
of ashes you left.
dusty dreams
frantic pressed
to gasping heart
to graying breast

❀ ❀

ON APRIL FEELING MORNINGS

on April feeling mornings
when sun
winks and dances
thru windows
to gently rock me
from soft dreams
to smooth dawn
and even the coffee pot
echoes the beat
I sing for you

in empty Sunday moments
in a small piece of corner
a small shriveling ball
called me
waits for the earth to
stop twitching
or explode

I used to scream for you
always you came
but though you tried
my empty corner
was much too occupied

despair is a passion
of solitude
How to share
when no one's there

I KNOW
you are
a hand a rock a waterfall
but also you're not there at all

a me
on April feeling mornings
needs
a hand a rock a you
to love

In 7 years

we will have
been together
for more than
half our lives

We even look
like each other
Gray hair, purple veins,
age freckles.
Are these things
contagious?
I know I never had any
before I met you.

I hope we make it
(i.e., live long enough to)

Because
I would have to say
Part II
has been
way better
than Part I
I think, the wisdom that
comes with aging
has something to do with it
But you have more

❋ ❋

THANKSGIVING 1998

I'd like to
thank

Everyone,

But
especially,

you

for fires, & fires
in the fireplace,
too

❋❋

Bankrupt

on our 10th
anniversary
financially

Rich on our 10th
anniversary
in every other
conceivable
way

Family & Friends

MOTHER

I lived for 9 months
        in her stomach

visions of 2 bedrooms
        (2 baths)
easily growing
        there
(Plenty of room

        in her womb)

One of the larger
                apartments

        I've ever had

lots of running water,

        too

❋❋

WW II

See this picture?

The pretty lady
with her hair
all up on top
of her head
is my mama.
& that skinny guy
in the soldier suit
with all those teeth?
He's my dad.

He lives in the army
far away
across the world
fighting & shooting
Nazis

He sends us these skinny
letters called V-mail

We send him
anchovies (ick)
& salamis

Mama, what's a war baby?

MOTHER

Oy! Be careful!
Oy, you'll slip
Oy, you'll fall

Until I was three
I thought my first name
was Oy

My sister has a friend who calls
my mother Mrs. Oy
If I call my mother
unexpectedly she says
Oy! What's the matter?!

For a long time my husband
was not allowed to call my mother,
because if he did it would
mean I was dead. (My husband
thought this was odd, but it
made perfect sense to me.)
Eventually, he was granted
permission, but he was carefully
instructed to say
"Diane's O.K.—Hi, this is Bill"
not
"Hi, this is Bill, Diane's O.K.,"
to which she would reply
"Oy, what's the matter?"

That last weekend we
all did the Sunday New York Times
crossword puzzle together
(actually, she did it,
        we just helped)

Saturday night
        we had a Seder
Ma had 1 matzo ball
        & lots of chopped liver

        Then, she said,
"I need to go to bed"

Easter Sunday morning
        we couldn't rouse her much
& by Monday morning
        she was dying.
I looked at her and said,
        "Oy, what's the matter?"
She opened her eyes &
        they said "Nothing, nothing is
the matter at all."
        She smiled, & then she was gone.
I called Jane right away & before
I could tell her she said
        "Oy! What's the matter?"

It was raining when

the soldier in the
picture
who everyone said
was my father
carrying a wet
green duffel bag

came home

❋❋

MEMORIAL DAY

I remember the day
my father came
home from the war
          carrying a big
                    green duffel bag

& I sat on the
couch between
          my parents &
                    said over & over
"my mommy *and*
my daddy"

then my mother
went into the kitchen
& I burst into tears
to be left alone
with a soldier
I didn't even know

❋❋

MOVING BLUES

We lived in Queens
in a very small flat
grandparents, 2 uncles, a new sister,
so that
some of us had to sleep on the settee
uncles, aunts, my sister & me

We looked at houses on Long Island
it seemed like forever
then mama said
it's now or never

I want this one
on Dogleg Lane
It's my dream house
the rest I disdain

My Dad said "Sure,"
I think we can make it
for $17,500
I think we should take it

& my grandparents said
"You've made your mark"
& I said, "Mama, we have our own park
I love it here. It is *so* nice
let's move in right now"
I didn't think twice

When I was 15
my dad lost his job
Had an offer in St. Louis
and it was very hard

My grandpa said
there wasn't a Jew
in all of St. Louis
—as far as he knew
He wasn't religious
he was a red
But I knew in St. Louis
we'd be better off dead

Dad kept singing
meet me in St. Louis
meet me at the fair
But we all cried
about going there

I never understood that movie
'cause they were all so sad
to move to N.Y.
like that would be bad

So he got a job in Newark
& we didn't have to go
We stayed on Long Island
forget St. Louis, MO

My father died 10 years ago
we never said thanks
But I like to think he'd know
He gave us all 5 hours a day
on the LI expressway
What more can I say?

COMMUNICATION

My grandfather
had a store
on 42nd & 7th Avenue

where he sold clothing 2nds

His store was frequented

by an above average
hearing & speaking impaired
number of individuals

How come so many

come here to shop?

Grandpa shrugged

I guess one tells
another

❃ ❃

Papa (my grandpa)
        loved soup
regardless of the season
        my sister's favorite
meal was lamb chops
        & scalloped potatoes
        in a blue ceramic bowl
& because it was her
        favorite, I insisted
                it was icky & refused
        to eat it
I could cry, now, when I think
of all the lamb chops I might
have eaten
        so I had hamburgers
instead
My dad ate Business
lunches at fancy restaurants
at 2 in the afternoon
& pushed his dinner
around on his plate
        My grandma had a
                hiatal hernia & although
she was not a picky eater
everything she ate
        got stuck
My uncle Bill put
ketchup on everything
& enjoyed raw onion sandwiches

GRANDFATHER

He was as tall
as clouds

& had to stoop
to catch
her secrets

He took her hand gravely
as they walked
and people smiled
to see them

He told her
bedtime stories
about Clarence Darrow
& taught her the names
of every senator
when she was 4.

They said the soldier
in the picture
was her daddy
in the war
But she didn't mind
because she had
the tallest grandpa
in the world

GUNYA

My grandmother
swore
that the first word
I ever said
(at 4 months old!)
was "Gunya"
This, in response to,
a picture that she
showed me
of her youngest son
my uncle Jackie
a merchant marine
in a white uniform
in 1943
then, so legend has it,
he came home on leave
& I, at 8 months only
took one look at him
& cried "Gunya!"
I almost think I remember this
& the incredible fuss
that followed

My mother called
the other day
& said they found
a spot
on his lung
can you believe it?
on Gunya's lung

But he was 6"4"
& tried out for the
NY Rangers
& ate whole rye breads
as fast as Jackie Robinson

If Gunya has a spot
on his lung
then things are not looking good
for the rest of us

GUNYA II

Well, we have reservations
(plane & otherwise)
to go to Washington
My mother, sister & me
to say goodbye
to Gunya

Who, as I reported
earlier,
was found to have
a spot on his lung

the trip is 3 weeks
away
& we pray
(or would,
if we did that
sort of thing)
that he'll be there
when we arrive
I'm not much for funerals

But I do think
It's good to say goodbye
to people
we love

The older I get,
the more
I say
goodbye,

(also
the older
all my friends
& relatives get)
One day
it will be me
that people will
have to say
goodbye to
&, I gotta say,
that,
no matter
what I look like
or, how bad I feel
(Hopefully, there will be
sufficient major drugs
to ameliorate the pain,)

I hope they do,

stop by,

to say
goodbye

HOT WATER BOTTLE

Hot water bottle
        red & smooth
                flannel nightgown
warm milk
        with butter & sugar
Toast cut into perfect
        little squares
Helen Trent
        &
        Our Gal Sunday

& a pillow

        of big, soft

                grandma arms.

ODE TO MY BIG SISTER

When my mother
(& yours too, I finally see)
accused you
of stealing
her TV clicker
(perhaps her control?
AHA!)
Did you snivel?
no
Did you feel guilty? no (well, a little)
Did you take drugs?
no
Did you never drive a car? no
Did you pout?
no

Did you get married 3 times?
NO
You told her to "cut the shit,
Mrs. Schizophrenic,"

You are my idol,
& I hope to grow up
& be just like you—some day

ATONEMENT

My sister
tells a story
(and tells it often)
about how
when I was 8
& she was 4
I brought home
these big chocolate
chip cookies
You could only get
at my school
and ate them in front of her
& when she begged me
to bring her some
or give her a bite
I said we weren't allowed to,
It was a school rule.
and she cried
& even though
I remember
nothing about
this alleged incident
I fear it is true
& I do most heartily atone
& beg her to forgive me
(& to stop telling the
damn story!)

We tossed

Uncle Bill
off a hill

of desert

in Las Vegas
as we approached
20 feet from the
edge
my mother
said
Oy, you'll fall off the ledge

❋ ❋

We went to
Las Vegas
To toss my uncle's
ashes

He loved to gamble
(He also enjoyed
a drink or 2
Well, actually,
he didn't *really*
enjoy it)

But he married
a WASP
(very nice but of course
she drank—& so, to
keep her company & to possibly save their marriage)
did he.

❋ ❋

MY CHILD

(OK   my stepchild
but the closest
thing I have)

is a born again
          Christian

& I
          am an atheist
          Buddhist
                    lapsed
          Jew
who loves Christmas
          the tree
                    the cookies
the presents
&
          most of all
the songs
& I'm afraid
she's missing
          the point
of Christmas
which is
to have a lot
of fun
& overdo

LABOR DAY

My aunt Jenny

was a union
        organizer
(The Ladies Garment Workers
        Union)

        I only met her
a few times

        she always was
                dressed in black

I thought she was
        the good witch
                of the North

&,
        she was!

Diane & Bill

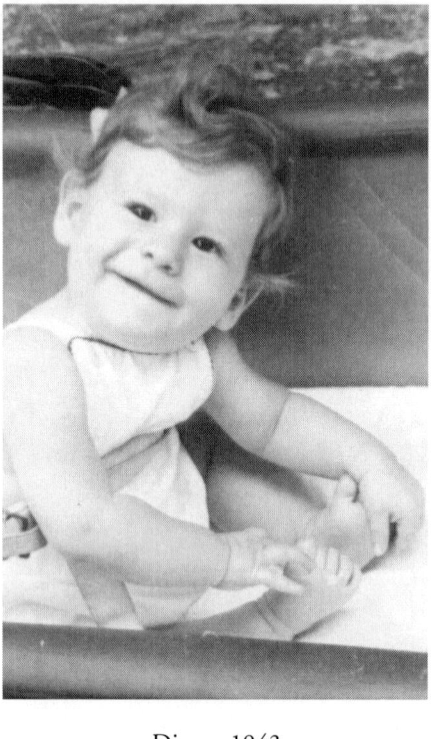

Diane, 1943

Jane & Diane, 1948

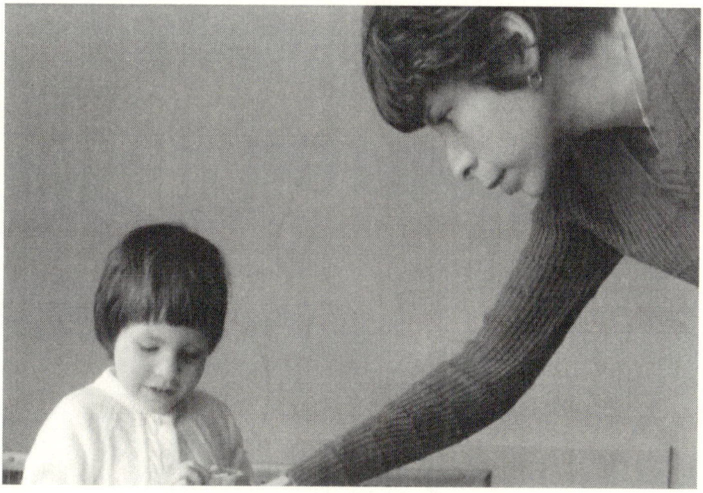

Diane & Gretchen

Dad, Diane, Mom, 1943

Diane, Gretchen, and Bill

Diane, 1946.

Diane, Gretchen, 1974

Jane, Diane, Dad, Mom, Roslyn Heights, NY—1963

Diane & Bill

Dad & Diane 1943

Mom, Dad, Bill, & Diane in 1974

Grandma Sophie, Diane, Grandpa Joe- Huntington, NY

Jane & Diane, 1947

Diane, friend and cousin Jeff-Huntington, NY

Diane in 1943

Sophie, Sam, Diane

Jane, Mom, & Diane in 1989

Bill, Diane, Sam & Sophie.

LAS VEGAS

Uncle Bill
        had several
albino qualities
so I hope
we did the right thing
tossing his ashes
        in the
        desert

Near as we could get
to his Heaven
We Christened him & toasted
him   with Johnny Walker Black
        & on the 7th day
                we rested

TO JEFFREY

who taught
me
what it's like
to be
a mother

you don't call

you don't write

you don't even have

a girl

& you look like
Joe Namath
& smart
& such a sense
of humor

You could be anything

Tonight

I made dinner
for a small
gray-haired

Woman
who
I've known
since we were
twelve
(her hair was chestnut
thick & curling)

How in the world

did
this

happen?

& what,
if anything,

did

happen?

a lot of nothing
a little
of everything

DEBBIE

A doe
caught in
the head lights
You clear your throat
and push up your glasses

But we're not fooled
for very long

for one thing
Your poems are a dead giveaway
for another
so are you

❦ ❦

ANGER

I am pretty sure

that Jerry Rubin

had imagined many endings

But, as he walked across

that street
in L.A.,

getting run over

by some poor guy
who maybe never heard of him

was not one of them

❈ ❈

Here's Jerry Rubin

of the 90s

marketing health drinks

making a buck

knowing he's on
a lot of lists
like the Attorney General's

& he's in a hurry
when he crosses
that street

and the guy who
hits him—maybe an angry
guy, too
Doesn't even know
who he is
Didn't have a contract
out on him
Just driving like we all do
maybe angry
Hits this other angry entitled jay-walking guy
& he dies—

Is there a lesson
here?
Bigger than anger
& politics

yes
& its name is
the scariest
of all—

impermanence

not a judgment
not a matter of power
or control

just the way things are

always

❋❋

MEMORIES

You probably won't believe this,

but;
at my husband's
insistence,
I called
L.A. information
for a listing
for
A Hal, or a Harold,
L or Lewis,
Ackerman.
They had one
just one
Who was listed twice

I called, & sure enough,
I got his machine
I could tell it was him
but I didn't—
leave a message

❋ ❋

As a person

of Jewish heritage

I,
along with others
of similar tendencies,
have been
very anxiously
awaiting
the Messiah
finally,
unto us,
he has come
take a guess—

Yes—
&
His name
shall be calleth
Michael Jordan
Prince of Peace
& 3rd highest
scorer
(so far)
in NBA history

HARVEY

If
You walk into
the dark forest

with people

for 23 years
eventually you
lose someone
no matter
how many
bread crumbs

you leave behind

❧ ❧

HARVEY

if only . . .
        what if . . .

I could have—

        I should have—

                I would have—

I really wanted

        to

(But
        I
        didn't)

❋ ❋

TO HARVEY

Softer than
wind chimes

Your bell tolled

whispering
despair

I wanted too
much
for you

❈ ❈

HALLOWEEN

I can't write
a poem about
Halloween

Pumpkins, candy
witches
Ho hum

once, though,
My date & I
went to a
Halloween party

as Donny & Marie
Osmond
& won the booby prize

❈ ❈

TO JOHN DENVER

Enough with the
eagles, John
they say that
you got crazy
& tried to touch the sun

When you leave
on a jet plane
you need gas

Eagles fly
in the Rocky Mountains
High
but people don't

or
if they do

they need a plane
& a plane
needs gas

TO LEE

So big deal
you had a shtick.

Everyone has something

Some people
gamble
or drink,
or take drugs
or hurt other people

All you did was
want to know
the word for
Shish Kebab
or
the name
of lake point towers

so I would tell you,
&,
in return
you taught me a little about Yiddish
& a lot
about love

Therapy

TO ROBERT

You laughed at my bolted door
        & opened it
(How'd you do that,
        anyway?)

& people have been
                dropping in
ever since

                which is nice
because I'm almost always
                home these days

❋ ❋

NON-LOVE POEM TO ROBERT

after lifetimes
        on planets
of blind men
        You
        flicked on the sun
(amused by
        my foolish
                nearsighted
                        act)
        & patting at

        my embarrassed
                sanity

❋ ❋

I said

I don't know
whether to be
          a poet
                    or a therapist
when I grow up
he said
          —well—
why not grow
up & be both
          at once
(now why didn't
          I
think of that)

❋ ❋

ROBERT

          x-ray
                    vision

saw it all
          & invited me
                    to have a
                              peek

takes my breath
                    away
          & gives it back

❋ ❋

ODE TO INTERNALIZING TRANSFERENCE

Hey
I know what the
third layer of
my cake is—
    it's you!

I thought I must have
fallen out of the nest—
there was a crack in
my shell—
so I came
& you laughed
& gently bludgeoned
the rest
    &
wobbly blinking at the
world I was
    & now

I'm learning to fly

❋❋

WOW

— — — —

before you fall out of the nest
you don't realize
    there is one
until you fall out, you don't
know there never was
a nest

❋❋

I always thought

my patience
    would expand
geometrically
    with my age
        & experience
Whew
    that was
        wrong
instead
    I find I have
almost zero
    tolerance
for most things
especially
    VICTIM
bullshit
I'm sitting there
& some person is saying
how
a lot of really bad
    stuff
happened to him
    &
I'm like
    yeah,
what's your point?
& they're like
    "well that . . .
        that's the point"
and I know I should say
"ah hah"
    or

"that is really hard"
        or
"so, tell me . . ."
        or
"It's really hard when bad
shit happens to you"
But what I find myself
saying
        more & more
is:
so, what your choice is:
1. Get a life
2. Shut up

❋❋

occasionally

        someone
will come into
        your office
& want
        to know
the truth
when that
        happens
you shouldn't interpret
        you
should tell them
as frankly
& gently
as you can

❋❋

musings

        & farts
from an old psychotherapist
        (OK—social worker,
        happy?)
why would a person
        spend 30 plus
                years
hanging out
        with a bunch
of crazy people?
there could be
                several reasons:
1. it makes them feel
not crazy or, at least
less so
2. they had a crazy depressed parent (or 2) & it was
their job to
        cheer up & make sane
                or
3. masochism is their
        kind of thing
                or
4. I don't know but
enough is enough

THE THERAPIST

I always like
the locker room
stuff,
afterward,
which explains
my choice
of profession

❦ ❦

I have been at
NW for almost 13
years—when Sandy Finkel came he
asked me how I
had lasted so long.
What was the secret?
I said, "Just keep
a low profile."
He said, "Oh, I
could never do that."
Psychodynamic
penchant leads to
this—11-month-old's
first sentence:
"Want to be
comfortable."
Revealing character pathology
many years of
expensive psychotherapy
have shown
the error of this
unfortunate habitual
pattern.

❦ ❦

I now

like clients
that have
similar problems
to mine

(I used to hate them)

I think this is
progress
for me, anyway

But I also must admit,
I'm a lot less
tolerant
of everyone else

including,
sadly enough,
those who have
problems
different from mine
luckily, there aren't any

❦❦

I've been
working at this job professionally
          for 30
                    years

& I can honestly
          say

I have
          no clue
as to how   to do
          this work

          & that
more than anything

          makes me
                    very good
                              at it
No one
          can tell you
          what to do
or how to do it
it's you & the tiger
& the cliff
& the strawberry

Because Dora's father

(not to mention
Herr K)

Were a bit intrusive
she
(silly girl)
fancied that
Dr. Freud
was
as well

This is called transference

(of course, he was)

This is called
reality

❋❋

My job as a "psychotherapist:"
I make friends
with a lot of people
that
no one else has
& see
how really nice &
smart & funny & SANE
these people are
& several of them
seem to be
getting the same impression

❋❋

lost it today

still

crazy after all these
years

& many hours
of expensive
psychotherapy
& even Prozac

❀ ❀

I have melted

into
the pit
of failure

I've managed
to avoid acknowledging
through denial,
adventure,
& modest
consumption
of various
substances
some
even
legal

But
        today
the shit hit
        the fan
& I am exposed
        as less than
                perfect

(I suffer from the
Good kind of
narcissistic personality

where,
        despite
                occasional
fits of entitlement,
I basically
        have no
                self
& therefore am more to be
pitied than scorned . . .

I wish it were true

that one thing
had nothing
to do with
the other

But it's not

one thing
has everything
to do with
the other

ADT

I just worked

eleven and 1/2 hours,
without a break,
(I should mention,
I am at the peak of
my wisdom—i.e.
much past
my midlife
crisis)
& deeply into
menopause
(Which, believe me,
when the air conditioning
doesn't work, & it's 95,

You better, the fuck,
stay out of my way)

But, I digress,
I was speaking of morale
& I gotta tell you
in the clearest, most precise
& proactive manner
I can muster
that
morale sucks

OK, wait

you're saying:

I work one in 3 Saturdays

with people who
I don't even know
who cut themselves
when they're having a so-so day
& worse, when things get
sort of bad
think suicide
is option number one,

so, wait,
& you're gonna pay me
my regular sucky hourly rate?

are you shittin' me?

Relationships

Shakespeare was right

About the stage
and relationships
allow a more
professional performance
if the casting is right
and it always is

❋ ❋

I don't

understand
all the
Goyim

never calling
each other
long distance

I don't understand
all the goyim
wasting every lovely
day

in SILENCE
I don't understand
all the goyim
eating white bread
& mayo
on corn beef
for Christ's sake

But they
quite enjoy it
so go
figure a
goy it
is one thing
I'll never
understand

People,

not unlike
onions,
peel

&
where there are onions
frequently,
there are tears
(also, where there are people,
frequently)

Paranoids

Don't
free associate
very well

obsessionals
make insomniacs
yawn

hysterics
spin the world
dizzy

passive aggressives
are always late
and drop
wine glasses
across a room

schizoids
aren't terrible
sociable

& narcissists
think
their oyster
is the world

NEIGHBORS

you
gathering still sore self
afraid of night
afraid of lights

shall win a place
among the flowers
surging swelling
stretching
toward
the sun . . .

and me
for trusting you could be . . .
a nearby daffodil.
perhaps
we shall greet
each other
then

mother's day

father's day

are sometimes painful

for the fertile

& the infertile
alike
(not to mention the children)
everyone
ends up
feeling
somewhat
wanting

like premature
ejaculation

or a sunset
at noon
or
raw nerve endings
pretending to be
relaxed

I feel very

Christmas-y

an odd state

admittedly

for an

atheist

Jewish

Buddhist

Let's face it
the goyim don't have
much going
foodwise or violinwise

but they do have
Christmas

❋ ❋

Autonomy

the relative goal

dependency
the path

or
are the
streets
paved with
intimacy
which is
nothing more
than
acknowledging
a fellow
pilgrim's
back

WHAT YOU DO

what you do
            matters
not   nearly
            so much
                        as
who you are
            in that hidden vault—
where lies   can't live
where eyes   swivel
            and focus
                        in,
and aren't fooled
                        at all

by
            what
                        you do

❈ ❈

aggression

slices thru love
ego's little tantrum
because
it's not
exactly like
we want to be

if you won't
let me consume you (share my
vision) I'll push you away
& find someone
who will

what ever happened
to opening?

(a year later) what ever happened

to love

❋ ❋

Rod McKewen
had it
all askewen

Love is

ALWAYS having
to say "I'm sorry"

❋ ❋

AFTER YOU LEFT

After you left
the hurt was a vulture
that lived in my stomach
and clawed, drawing blood
and I thought the worst had come

But after the bird
had aged   and withered
parchment stiffened
dead and heavy
I thought the worst had come

And now that the corpse
is decomposing
          too filled with decay
          to dream a different day
I know the worst has come

CHILDREN

can my friend, well . . . 3,
        come for dinner
tonight?

        Great,   thanks
                oh

I forgot to tell you
        Sarah is a lacto
                vegetarian

& Sean has a lacto
        intolerance

& Jessica has an eating
        disorder—anorexia or
        bulimia
                I forget which

So anyway we'll get home
at oh 6:00 or 8:00?

                or, we may eat

                        at Sarah's

Go to the
head of the class

Suppose you don't
want to?

Then there must

be something

wrong with

you

(or with going

to the head

of the
class)

Dogs

What a good:

Sophie
meat loaf, Sophia
Sophie loafy, Sophella
loaf cake
Missy, precious face,
Mrs. Pisher,
girly,
girly girl,
Baby girl, sweet meat,
Love girl—

Crash—

❋ ❋

They left me alone all day & I ate the kitchen
They were mad but guilty so . . .
"This is Sam," they said,
I wagged my tail (it was
expected) & took a sniff
        Whew, this guy needed
a bath!
        He approached me
                in a respectful crouch
                tail between his legs
I lay down, yawning
very bored
        & with a sigh of relief
He curled up with me
        his bony hips
                Poking me

And they
        clucked & beamed
                so I let him
                stay

Now he lives here
        Too
& gets braver by the day
running under me &
biting my legs &
behaving like a puppy
& I stay home with him all day
        to baby-sit

SAM'S SONG

I was found
          in the pound

He came to get a cat
But he saw me
and that was that

He called her to say
that he had found a stray
          A dog not a cat
& what did she think of that?

she said, we've always wanted a son
& it sounds like you
have surely found the one

a Sam to be our Sophie's brother
a fine boy puppy for me to mother

they both adored me
though Sophie seemed bored
not that she bit me
But I felt ignored

In the last few years
though it seemed
a lot more sudden
Sophie the dog
got old
& more & more
she laid around
& thumped
a few times

Wednesday
she died
But here's my plan
whenever I pass her spot
I'll act like
she's
still there
it won't be all that hard
now I finally
understand
why people
choose psychosis
over reality
sometimes
it is
the lesser
of two evils

In the pound they almost

put me to sleep
But then he found me
and I knew I was theirs to keep

Years later Sophie died
& they were very sad
But they still had me
and I was secretly glad

Now I'm old
one hundred and two
and there is still so much
I want to do

Mostly eat
whatever is near
&, on occasion,
have a beer

And prance with him
and cuddle with her
& live to be a ripe old cur

But soon I'll die
Getting ready to go
I hope they'll be OK
But . . . I don't know

❋❋

SAM

Your face
tried to look brave
But your body was shaking
& gave you away
I led you
out of that sad place
& you sat
shivering
on my lap
in the car
we introduced you
to Sophie
in the parking lot
like they said we should
she seemed bored
and then
          we all went home
You were so thin
Your hip bones showed
You inhaled the food we gave you
& curled up
          next to Sophie
who still looked bored
& you purred a dog purr
& went to sleep
we roasted a duck
& I knew
today was the best day

SAM & I

We were home
Alone
You were away & Sophie was dead
& I remembered that day
We walked him
Out of the
Pound—proud & terrified
& how he shook
on my lap
in the car
driving home

& he & Sophie
introduced
in the parking lot
& how he laid up
against her
eyes darting
"Is this OK?"
& after, he had a bath,

stood there
frozen & resigned
& we all smelled the
duck
roasting in the oven

& Sam
crept in
several circles
& lay down on the red
blanket
(His red blanket, but he
couldn't believe it yet)
& I knew,

as I looked
at you

That today
was one of the best
days.

❋❋

My wife (husband)

is a very
unusual person
for example
she (he) soul kisses
our dog
(it's not that I don't but she/he started it)

❋❋

HERE SAM

Come 'ere SAM
Sammy! Come!
Oh
NO

❋❋

The bearded vet came
Put our dog Sophie to sleep
The house is empty

❋❋

Does a dog have
        Buddha nature?
Does a person?

❋ ❋

The old dog's

        legs twitch

Wonder what
        he dreams about
Prob'ly bones

❋ ❋

DOG

Can't cry
for Sophie

if I start I'll never stop
(start & never ever stop)
Where is my girl now?

❋ ❋

SOPHIE

Half the people
I've loved in my life

are dogs.

(The rest are cats,
except for you)

❋ ❋

MY DOG SAM

Is so old
that his legs
Give out
& he slips &
goes
splat

on the floor
& can't get up
so he lays there & yowls
& I,
weighing about
as much as he does

can't help him

get up
so, I start yowling, too

❋ ❋

SAM

I got home
tonight

& no one
barked,
or gave
a welcoming

Yowl,

& I realized
you were really gone
although
I still can't
believe it.

❦ ❦

Old black dog is gray

she can barely
thump her tail
Hardly,
anymore

❦ ❦

SOPHIE

Having only had
puppies

& not being a dog

(although the word bitch
has been used
to refer to
this writer)
I can only say
that my children are
seven-score & more
& will probably

pre-
decease
me.
& everyone says
losing a child
is the hardest.
I think,
that goes
for mother dogs,
also.

SOPHIE

I had a dog
that got old
& gray & grizzled

She slept most of the day
with only a thump
of her tail
here & there
when I walked by,
except,
once in a while
her eyes got a puppy gleam
& she pointed at a
green tennis ball
& dove & captured
her prey
& proudly shook it
to display
& limped home, smiling.

FIRST KISS

Gazing into my eyes
your first kiss
was tentative
as if you expected me
to pull away

when I did not
your confidence
Grew
& there was no place
anywhere
on my face
you did not kiss
each kiss growing
wetter & more passionate
until you began to
nibble on my lips
with needle teeth
& I had to say
no bites, bad dog,
just kisses

The golden retriever
                points at the
        car's trunk
where her
        Christmas presents
                are hidden

(or so we thought)

we went to Pet Smart
(notice they don't call
        it "People Smart")

❋ ❋

Just go on in there

& TAKE IT
that's all
        it's yours
        after all
come on
        get down from
under the table
        & stand up
                &
take your seat

❋ ❋

Sophie, don't eat the fireplace, please

My idea of
disciplining
        a dog
                Is
to say
"Sophie" (that's my dog)

"Please don't"
                please

❈❈

PUPPY POEM

On the paper
        that's a good girl
No
        No
                No!
on the *paper*

❈❈

SOPHIE

I just want to
fill my eyes
        up with her
we got some
extra time
        I thought
                was gone

appreciation
        should never
be squandered

❀ ❀

Dog Love

        is so pure
& so contrived
(kind of like
        people love)
only done better

❀ ❀

My mother

crochets
beautiful afghans
of multi-colored squares
sewn together
She made one
with green & purple
wool that I loved

so did my dog Sophie

she thought it looked
good enough to
eat

which she did

I heard

you all
were
writing poems

from someone else's
point of view

like mostly
your animal friends
& apparently
Sam
wants us all to believe
that he wrote this poem
(that rhymed!)
Well
the mutt has
one advantage:
He's alive
he can hunt or play or
run into the rain
He never sees
a tennis ball
or brings one home
But
I understand
he wrote
a so-called
poem
about how
he was
the favorite
& most-loved dog
& was
glad

when I died
Well—all I can say
is

You'll get yours

soon enough

❦ ❦

CHANGES

I was standing in front
of the office building
where I work
on a cloudy Monday
morning in October
when a poodle
I had never met
stopped to say hello
& gave me
a big wet kiss

then proceeded on his way

❦ ❦

eyes sparkling

chest heaving
ears perking
tail pointing

pounce!

proudly displays
the spoils

not a tennis ball
her usual prey

but the
prize of
the hunt

a soccer ball!

❋ ❋

I live with

        a very big
part Doberman
        part Great Dane

        Dog
named Sam

        in the subs

& this dog

        (weighs 100 lbs.)

is scared to go out

        into the fenced-in yard
                alone
        after dark

so I go with him

& I say,
"It's OK, Sam,
        don't worry,
        it's OK,"
(But I wonder—is it?)

Condo

You know how

I like
a bargain

a suit
on sale
re-sale
shop
I know you can't
get something
for
nothing

but surely
you can
get something
for less
except
in the
mondo
of condo
where you bargain
up
on a piece of merchandise
that doesn't fit

❃ ❃

MORTGAGE SHOPPING

Do you know
what
a
Balloon payment
is?
Neither did I
'til recently.
It's just what it
sounds like.
A payment
that gets
bigger
and bigger
and bigger
'til it pops
and you
go
Bankrupt!

❋ ❋

I've bought some things
        before
a 3-piece suit
        &
Calvin Klein jeans
(size 6, 8, & alas, 10)

        even a dining room set
(second hand, but still)

today we looked at
        condos
10 of them
        &
I felt like an American
        dizzy
with possibilities
(the one we can't afford
        was the one I wanted)

still
        if we never
                eat out
                        again
& take bag lunches
it could be ours

But who
        would
                we be?

When I go to the grocer
I squeeze the avocados
But this has not prepared
me
properly
for mondo condo
I do
of course
squeeze & jiggle
the toilet flusher
count the closets
lay
spread eagle
in the kitchen

While my husband
feels radiators
& searches for outlets

There were these four
we saw
that, with a little work . . .
I never thought
this would happen
to me
(or at least
you)

but here we are
talking mortgages
& tuck points

BULL

While their interest rises
our interest wanes

The goys jew the Jews
The preacher preaches
the chirping
parents
preen
prematurely

and the house
comes
tumbling
down.

❋ ❋

We made an offer
and thought we were done
looking at condos
one
by
one

But another couple came along
and our offers
and counter-offers
must have been wrong
for they got the place
or so we hear
end of the race
wipe a tear

Bad enough
you well may say
But tomorrow will be
a bright new day
of
looking at
condos

All the king's horses

and all
the king's
men
Can't seem to
work up
Humpty Dumpty's
enthusiastic peeps
or ours
as we enter
into
Day Three
of
negotiations
for the condo
soon to be
ours
or theirs
and you know
what happened
to him

MONDO CONDO

I suppose
        everyone
        has a dream house
mine is made
        of Cape Cod
                shingles
a fireplace
        in the bedroom
                too

with ocean
        the only neighbor

                or

a brick condo
        close to
                a great lake
        would be
                a reasonable
                        settlement
tuck pointing
        has its place
in the real world

Entering the world

of
Mondo Condo
with
earnest (money)
We made an offer
on a condo
that wasn't quite
what we wanted
and was
quite
what we could afford
O.K.
I know it's very small
but we should be glad
it's there
at all
and then
Another couple made
an offer
larger than our own
just how much larger
we cannot know
We upped ours
of course
(What did you expect?)
and now
we are bidding
for a place
we don't really want
with an unknown
hateful
couple

and it seems
disloyal
to almost
hope
they get it.

P.S. They did.

❋❋

Remember the place

we didn't
get

Well now
they want us
to have it
But we didn't
want it
anymore.
We found a better one
(ha ha)
and we got it
(I think)
and
All's well
that ends well
if we only
qualify for a mortgage
it will be ours!
Or the bank's
if you want to
get technical

❋❋

MONDO CONDO II

We saw ten condos
today
none was perfect
some had potential
but which?
was it
the second
or the fourth
the eighth
had a mean
tenant
who kept turning
the lights off
the sixth
(or was it the seventh)
was too small
but had
a great kitchen
my head
is spinning
on my neck
like a top
or a dreidel
the American dream
I'd always supposed
was surgically removed
or never there
(a birth defect
no doubt)
is
twingeing
in a forty-year-old
uterus
(OK—forty-one)

retarded
but
rearing
it's Mongoloid head
the fourth place
had a sweet porch
the 3rd
or was it
the 4th?
had 2 bathrooms
(talk about heaven
& the 9th was too)
small . . .
still
a lake view
can be squeezed into
nothing perfect
all possible
let's rent
for another year

We made

an offer
today
on a condo
I never thought
I'd see the
day
(in quite this way)
although
God knows
I've made offers
before
& to be fair
had a respectable number of
offers myself

I'd rather

get married
lots of times
(and have)
than buy
a condo
(what's the difference
between a
condo
&
a husband?)
You can
get rid of
a husband

❋ ❋

The Summer of '84

offered
conventions
&
good intentions
Olympics
too
(though poorly attended)
But most of all
when we think back
we'll remember
condos
big ugly condos
small thin attractive
condos
bland
condos
condos with fireplaces—
wood burning (we can check
& see if it works)
window treatments
are negotiable
as are mortgages
as are points
as are we

A CHILD OF THE SIXTIES

ending war
seemed the chore
to spend
all energies on
smoking dope
the only hope
now it's 1984
& we
(yes—you & me)
are on the brink
of buying a condo
What happened?
Have hopes of peace
become a place
to entertain
friends?
can a built-in bookcase
replace
sophomore dreams?
yes
especially if it has
a wood-burning
fireplace

Who would have believed

the relief

that came with
the (why is it taking so long?)
news

that we passed the ultimate test:

the dreaded
credit check

(not that we had anything
to worry about)

we owe thousands of dollars

clearly
our credit
is exemplary

Nature

THE GREY LAKE

TOLD ME A POEM

TODAY

ABOUT WINTER

❋❋

VERMONT

Fall leaves a rainbow
Red yellow & orange gold
look there look at that

❋❋

IT'S SNOWING

It's snowing
I think

just gently now
until
a wind gathers
and swirls

into
a blizzard

exploding now:
a SNOW CYCLONE spinning
everything into NOW

and

very later

softly slides

& scatters

windy echoes &
whispering white flakes

it stopped snowing
i think

LIGHTS

Coated up for winter
        bus people
                look down
not seeing
                it's
        just dawn

& someone
        has
finger painted the sky
        with red
                & purple
        lights

❊ ❊

Sunset

purple
red

& pink
fingers

paint the sky

fading misty
orange, now

dropping softly
into the sea

❈ ❈

HARVEST

September
in the afternoon

saddle shoes
crunching
yellow leaves

new pencil smells

tomatoes
bursting
on window sills

❈ ❈

Burning leaves

& pencil smells
shiny lunch box
& plaid corduroy dress
too excited
to go
to sleep
walking on
crunchy yellow leaves
to the orange school bus
crisp blue sky
after sleepy summer

SOUNDS

sea sounds
at dawn
gulls playing
hide & seek

their laughter

crackles
as waves ripple
clouds whisper

sun

a pink embryo

waits

to be born

❋❋

BRIDGES

A thin bridge
of pink
sunlight
connects cloud mountains
one to another

as the morning lake
proclaims

autumn's first day

❋❋

AUTUMN

Even dirty

Bus windows
can't dull

red purple
October mornings

recalling smells
of pencils
newly sharp

& a boy

with tan
crew necked
covered
shoulders

❋ ❋

Our living room

is filled
with
smells
of the lake
Imagine
being so near
that
blue wet water
settles
around your furniture
&
turquoise breeze
kisses
your everyday
life

snow is pretty

snow is nice
but often snow
turns into ice

WINTER

Christmas is silver

silver stars

dot the black

night sky

melt into
a pewter morning

bare trees
point toward
the green silver lake

Michigan Avenue
is tinsel
& winking silver lights
&
crystal snow flakes
fall from
the gray
silver
sky

❀ ❀

Morning excites me

a certain dew
        on everyday things
a crisp building
        a dusty bus window
                teasing
half-forgotten
memories

❋❋

MOON

Sometimes barely there

sometimes silver
        round sky light

I'm a lot like you

❋❋

Leaves like

        Golden Hands

swirl on the

        porch

another autumn

        morning

❋❋

STORM'S AFTERBIRTH

hands
in casual behind-back clasp
for taking stock after the hurricane
nodding at
a branch here
a shingle there
stooping to right
an old porch chair
(not carried off, then
sure it had been)
wind so strong
storm so long
eyes skimming see
a hard-loved acorn tree

wrong where it was
just as well
it fell

❋❋

RAIN

It's early in the
morning

& it's raining
wet streets
hold promises
of getting into the world
somehow
together again

❋❋

LEAP YEAR

If you asked me
(which no one did)
when to add
an extra day
You can bet
it wouldn't
have been in February.
Why not
a rose-filled
day in June
instead?

❈ ❈

The apple tree
Groaning and drooping
With the weight
Of winter snow
Awaits impatiently
A green blue time
In the center . . . himself,
(Groaning and drooping
with apples)

❈ ❈

SEASONING

Alone
        with pride & pain, or crooked axis
        rotation is accomplished
(it's like they say
night follows day)
a certain symmetry here
        wanting now
                the syncopation
                        of seasons

Together
        we could heat
                things up
        & try our hand
                at
        revolution

GOD'S ODD SATURDAY

god did nice work
with water & light
& so forth
up thru that fifth day—
should have stopped then—
but—
being that there
is nothing greater than,
went on and did his narcissistic thing
when Sunday came he viewed his handiwork
and now
well he's not dead
or resting
he's just depressed

❋ ❋

I can't tell

which is louder

        Ella
or the
waves

—either way

❋ ❋

LISTENING

The sound of the sun
rising red
over the lake

The echo of the fog
hugging the gray water

The whisper of snow
falling white
& soft

The pink & yellow
choir
of rosebuds
opening

❋ ❋

The green lake

told me
a poem today
about rain

"poetry as a path
to peace"

Haiku

what I'd really like
to do
is write
a haiku
that said it all
in just three lines

❋❋

the purple crocus
peeks out from under the snow
isn't it spring yet?

❋❋

show me a crocus
purple velvet bursts through mud
I'm a fool for April

❋❋

the broken umbrella
lies helpless against the tree
catching stray raindrops

❋❋

DESIRE

a seagull floats in
to a wave in the ocean
your eyes are so green

❋ ❋

OCTOBER SKIES

red, pink, orange, rose
October sky at sunrise
good to start the day

❋ ❋

ENDINGS

red & purple clouds
sun falling into the lake
Michigan sunset

❋ ❋

pristine gleaming white
turning into graying slush
winter in Chicago

❋ ❋

amazed by the sky
pink & silver ribbons
gift wraps green blue world

❋ ❋

the squirrel & crow
argue beside the dumpster
who will be victor

❋❋

gray Winter light fights
with yellow forsythia
who will win?

❋❋

the daffodils stand
at attention awaiting
a signal to march

❋❋

look, the first green buds
popped out while we were sleeping
I wanted to watch

❋❋

DREAMS OF SPRING

Purple Hyacinths
insinuate their noses
up through the gray snow

❋❋

Lilacs spilling through
slats in rough wooden fences
windy perfume spray

❈ ❈

white borrowed tulips
in a tall blue & white vase
they will be perfect

❈ ❈

we make our choices
I don't like the video
win a few & lose

❈ ❈

my neck really hurts
like a jackhammer moved in
took up residence

❈ ❈

come & see the bluebird
sitting on the lotus branch
oops too late he's gone

❈ ❈

cherry blossoms fall
like snowflakes on new Spring grass
and then they are gone

❋❋

just before the storm
the ferocious black dog crept
under the table

❋❋

there was a green couch
all the grownups were crying
FDR was dead

❋❋

wet misty pavement
soldier with green duffel bag
home from the war

❋❋

my baby sister
all she did was cry & sleep
I'd prefer a dog

❋❋

cotton candy clouds
boat cradle rocking softly
sunset on Duck Lake

❋ ❋

I want to be
kissed by a dolphin
I want to deserve it

Poetry

I feel the unpublished poems
                    once again
coursing through my blood

          after a long
& premature retirement:

          a flower—
                    an ocean—
                              a poem—

❋ ❋

I used to worry
          about
          running out of
                    poems
Then I worried
                    they would
          choke me
& I would not last long
                    enough
          to make them all

Now I fret
          occasionally
about one
                    or the other
          but mostly
          I write poems

❋ ❋

Who ever thought
I'd run out of
paper
Before I ran
out of poems

❋ ❋

Poems
Vomit
can't stop them
don't want to

❋ ❋

I had a poem
& I lost it
it was really
a good one, too.
shit
I hate when that happens

❋ ❋

I have an endless
supply
of poems
which is why
I hope
I don't die
too soon

❋ ❋

My father
always said
that shorthand
& typing

should be
learned

He was right

penmanship

can't keep
up

with
poems

❋❋

I now know
that whatever happens
(& it probably will)
that
I'll
never
run out of poems

❋❋

I thought of
the best
fuckin'
poem
ever
& then I
forgot it

Damn!

❋❋

There are more poems
than anything else

there's space

all the rest
is
poem

❋❋

ANTIDEPRESSANT POEM

I'm having such a good
time
I don't want it to end

why should it
have to?

no reason
no real reason

Here we are
after all
&
all the rest
is humor

Poems are

    eternal

Good ones,
    &
    bad ones,

    or,
they're
    impermanent,

& so is
    everything else

    good ones
    &
    bad ones

I'm doing this
          expressive therapy
                    meditation seminar
where people will
          sit & write
& one of my favorite
          people
          in the world
was scared to come
so I tried to reassure her:
You won't be on the spot
the lines people write are
anonymous—
                    etc.
                              etc.
But I forgot to tell her
that whenever I pick
          up a pen
I feel like my
          life is
                    at stake
& sometimes every line I write
is a razor, in a shaky hand,
the tiger has me over the cliff
hanging by a root
          that is coming undone
oh—there's a strawberry—
or a poem—I guess I'll have it . . . .
          now

Ever feel a song
penetrate
so you
& it
are one
each other?
Ever make
love to
a poem?

❈ ❈

A poem

is
a way of
touching
a flower
(or dancing
with a cloud)
or naming
a moment
or hugging
the
sky

❈ ❈

Hi,
I'm having
    a nice
        time—
I'm writing
    poetry,
    on the toilet—
It's where
    I do
        my best
    work

❋ ❋

The thing about
    writing poetry
once you
    really get
        started

        is

you fall in
    love
        with
            every word
& fuck
the whole
    thing up

❋ ❋

The only good thing
about chronic
pain
is
that it makes you
want to write
a lot more
poetry
The bad thing
is
you would
trade
every
poem
for a moment's
relief
(well, no,
not every
poem)

❋❋

I probably
have
1000 more
good poems
to write
But I think that
I'm done
for tonight

❋❋

Here's an idea for

the best poem ever written

OOPS

No pen or paper

❋❋

She said,
"Poetry Magazine
didn't think much
of 'personal poems,'"

"But all my
poems
are personal,"
said I.

"Yes
I know,"
she said.

"Well, maybe that's
why they never published
any of the poems
I submitted,"
said I.

"Well," she said
"That may be one
of the reasons."

❋❋

THE POETRY GROUP

Whenever I write a poem
I'll think of you
of you, Mary,
Becoming a giraffe
before my eyes
of you, Ian,
& golden years
of pewter poems
of you, Betty
bare beautiful
Haiku bones
of you, Sari
weaving sonnets
of Eastern shores & golden boys
of you, Juan
making music & storms
into poems
of you, Susan
Daring a poem
to be born
And June, Fritzie & Harvey
&
Gerry, Royce & Edna
& even Frida
Whenever I write a poem . . .

misty pink & orange
circle endings

One thing
I really like to do
is write
good poems

I also enjoy
being funny
so everyone
smiles

mostly
it's good
to hang around
with people
trying to
get sane

I wouldn't mind
having thin legs, either

❋ ❋

I need
the poet's
equivalent
of newsprint—
yellow legal pads
to fuck
full of
poems

❋ ❋

We play with
our minds
& sit with
our minds
& fuck
our minds
so why not
"write
our minds."

making a poem
isn't all that
different from

making love

You have a mind—

write it!

❋ ❋

On the day
I realized
the poems
would never stop
knowing
all the while
an unknown rhythm
rules
their birth
on that day
I relaxed

❋ ❋

I've written some poems
I really thought
were
terrible
and others
protest
politely,
& rightly
I've also
written
some poems
I knew
were
my children
& others
have coughed
Embarrassment
seems the
permanent
state
of the poet

❋❋

Lately
Whenever I get
                suicidal
(about twice a week)
        It seems
                like being
                a poem
                        abortionist
                so—I decide—
                        to
                                have the poem
                                        instead

❋❋

I don't believe
        in things
        that easily

        But
                there is
                        one thing
        I know
                is true

                That anyone
I don't
        care who

        can
write
                a
                poem
Why not you?

❋❋

Letting panic
pump itself
thru my veins
not stopping it

undercutting with
a question mark

laughter
kissed by compassion

writing a poem

❦ ❦

Good poetry
    is just
        regular talk
    only
        shorter

❦ ❦

The poetry lady
        weaves sonnets
as old as the lake

as young as a crocus

The poetry lady
        sells the truth
(at bargain rates)

The poetry lady
        brings gifts
        when it isn't even Christmas

The poetry lady
invents the light
        christens the moment

& names our lives

The real poems
are
born
from eyes
& skin
ears & noses,
also,
& toes,
I suppose
& livers
gall bladders too

real poems
burst
out of
anywhere

❈❈

a poem
a day
keeps the
psychiatrist
away

❈❈

I don't jog
but I do
write poems

I guess I'm not
a yuppie
after all

❋❋

I just wrote
a poem
that tells
the truth
in the fewest
possible words
& I feel,
for a second,
everything

❋❋

I may not
be good
as, say,
Edna St. Vincent Millay

❋❋

IMPERMANENCE

I wonder
what
the last poem
will say?

I guess that
partly depends
on whether or not
it's known to be
THE LAST
or just thinks
it's one more
in a long line

I think If I knew
it was the last
I couldn't write it . . .

—be good,
if I could—

but talk about
pressure

I haven't written

what I consider
          to be
a really good poem

in a very
          long time

so I write
          shit like this

just to keep
          my hand in

❈❈

The poems
          are pouring
                    out
of my
          whatever

they come from

& I gotta say

          I'm exhausted

❈❈

TIME

It's 2 a.m.
But try
telling that

to a

poem

❦ ❦

If you
are lucky
enough
to be adored
by a poet person

You will have
several

love poems
written
praising
your many charms

if not
you won't

❦ ❦

There are so many
                    poems
to write
                    I wonder which ones
will emerge
                    tonite?

❋❋

I just felt like
                    reading
                    all my old
                              Poems

& then,
                    I thought,

why not
          write
          a new one
                    instead?

❋❋

make poems
          not wars

❋❋

I've written

poems
about
gum problems
& horrible
invasive
procedures
& buying condos
& losing
that last
6 lbs.
But,
I've never written
a "giving up
smoking"
poem
before.

Health & Aging

POST HYSTERECTOMY POEM
OUCH

❋ ❋

FIBROIDS

Fibroids
I never even
thought about fibroids

malignant melanoma
yes
Brain Tumor
sure

But fibroids?

I've heard of androids
dated a few
Even behaved like one
on occasion

Who knew?
a post-menopausal uterus & ovaries
don't do that much
but take them out
&
it hurts

❋ ❋

GETTING OLDER

Getting older
    is eating
    4 chocolate chips
        straight
        without the cookie
    &   thinking
        you've had
            dessert

Getting older is
    having whatever
        you want
    but less than
        you used to
    & not really wishing
            you could
                have more

    except in a
        bittersweet
            way

    that is

        obliterated

    by heartburn

GUMS

gums
        by gum

Probably never gave
        them
        much thought

        legs, yes

        waist, yes

        gums, no

        until
                they go

Now I know,

        what is life?

                gums

FRENCH FRIES

I've given up chocolate
    steak & cream
Butter & sugar
    seem like a dream

But there's still one thing
    I can't resist
French fries dripping with grease
        but crisp

If in heaven I end up
    (to my surprise)
I just know it is made of
    crisp salty french fries

I had a friend who
    adored french fries
she said to apply them
    direct to the thighs

    about my weight,
        I don't tell lies
& I've gained 10 pounds
from eating french fries

Temptation can come
    in many a guise
But for me it begins & ends with
        french fries

The nice thing
about
Alzheimer's

is
You don't mind
summer reruns
anymore

❋ ❋

LOWER GI

Everyone was very nice
except for me
But I was the one
with the barium
where God never meant
it should be

Finally I thought
we were there
but then they said
"& now, for some air"

Just 3 passes left
& we'll be done
be sure to get the right side
It's my best one

❋ ❋

When I was
    young
    I needed sex

to know
    I was

    now
        a heating pad

    or an ice pack

functions
    in a similar
        manner

Getting in shape

has never

made much
sense
to me

In shape for what?

for death?

that seems silly

for what else, then?

I don't believe there is
anything
else

❋ ❋

I think there are way too many spots
on way too many people's
lungs
especially,

in my family,
well, many were smokers,
OK they all were smokers
I'm one, too,
& I haven't a clue
what to do

Replacement therapy
        as it is
euphemistically called
means you have
        PMS & periods
deep into menopause
        not to mention cramps
what you don't have
        is osteoporosis
& heart disease

        a fair trade?
                I guess so

But being PMS-y

can be messy

        & I am
                as we speak

Wallowing

what I'm really
waiting for,

          is the day

I give up,
          giving up,

smoking

another
        new year

they're mounting
up,
as are the resolutions,
never did one,
not once,
So this year
I resolve
not to make
any

getting old
        has its
                advantages

wisdom vs.
        arthritis

who will win?

        so far
arthritis
        has a definite
head start

❋ ❋

TRUE STORY

OK,
You just had all your
front teeth pulled
& the temporary bridge
(I know why they call it that)
doesn't fit too well
& causes you "discomfort"
& your 78 year old mother
is having cataract surgery tomorrow
& your gynecologist first told you
today that a hysterectomy is
indicated
sooner rather than later

A day
at a
time?
are you
kidding?

We are talking

a millisecond
at a time,

or
less.

E.R.

"Yes, Doctor, a 52 year old
woman in exam room 4—
X-rays indicate a
fractured patella"
        Wait! That's me
Oh NO! Oh my God
        Am I a
                52 year old woman?

❋ ❋

A broken patella
But,
        What the hell-a?
sounds like a deal
never even heard
        of a patella
can't be much
        Well—wrong!
it's a knee cap, is
what it is—
        something no leg
should be without
& they put you in a cast
from the ankle
        to the ass
& as your leg swells
& the cast cuts into
your flesh
        you try to
catch up on your
reading
but your concentration
isn't what it should
be & then
you have to take
        a piss
(Did I mention
you were a woman?)

How many are the
patella
poems
a person can
produce?

The possibilities
are plentiful

a plethora
perhaps

finally,
        my very first
                law suit

I have an
actual case
everyone says so
        negligence
prior incident reports
        floors waxed to
                a dangerous sheen
all add up to
        limited range of motion
                mental anguish
        lost revenues
thoughtless destruction of what
was probably the
most
adorable knee caps
in the continental
United States
Plus
        seriously interfering
with a safe &
moderate exercise plan
        (walking)
that the patient was
fully committed to,
& about to begin
the very next day
following the
unprovoked &
malicious events

LAW SUIT II

So we met with
the "slip & fall"
          lawyer
& he kept saying
"So, when you fell
down, when you fell
down & went boom" or
something
A grown man,
But he thought we
          had a case
"Hey, I don't take
schlock cases, OK?"
I don't know whether to be
humored or insulted

❋ ❋

I just glared at
          my legs

they puckered
          back at me

          Hmmm
                    not so bad
                    not what they once were
                              but
                                        not so bad

❋ ❋

I peeked
down the neck
of my nighty
& saw
breasts pointing toe-ward
& a stomach
resting on
a dimpled
thigh

I no longer need
to wonder
where has it all gone

so this is what they mean
by six feet
under

Giving up

smoking

has made me

write a lot
more poems

than
falling in
love

ever did.
(of course,
if you are
in love,
you're pretty busy

fucking)

❋ ❋

It's hard enough
to give up
smoking
without
a sore neck
that won't
ever
go away

of course
though
that's what

made me
do it

I'm getting the
idea
that some stuff
never goes away

I found a hair
today

it was gray

& it wasn't
on my head
(if you take my meaning)

I grow old . . .
oh well
a gray hair
is better
than none

that's next
you lose your hair

from everywhere
& it all grows

back
on your chin

I used to think
I'd never have hairs
growing
from my chin
now I think

When I do

I'll tweeze them
Another twenty years

I may decide

to keep them

or forget

they're there

OSTEOPOROSIS

I'm not
supposed,
to even have

a diet coke!

They have taken
everything

I ever cared
about,

away,

except,

you.

twelve is
    the first dry hump
    & how good it feels
        &
    Playing with dolls
        in secret
    & pink lipstick
        & the red
blood
of a woman
& hamburgers with fries
& first stirrings
    of questions

    & falling in love

❋ ❋

twenty-two
    is
    Swanson's chicken pot pies
        and
        the Peace Corps
            &
        embarrassment
            &
    fondue sets
    & cake mixes
        & hesitation
    & meatloaf
        & Black Russians
    & clitoral orgasms
        self induced

& fear
& basement apartments
in dangerous places
& blindness
& sweet & sour meatballs
in a chaffing dish
& questions

❋ ❋

42 is
a gray streak
a body that
spreads
when you lay
down

a brain,
whose cells
explode & die
as we speak

a fat
satisfied
cat

a glimpse of
how much more
there is to know

❋ ❋

lately

as middle age
embraces me
I've had the most
peculiar cravings
to get healthy

surely it will pass
but I find myself

pouring
wheat germ on things
having exercise fantasies
wondering what it
would be like
not to drink

(I'm not going to
give up smoking,
though)

I get occasional
glimpses
of my face
in mirrors
in sunlight
without makeup
—often I count
the wrinkles
—on some occasions
now & then—
I love

sometimes
I don't

❈❈

Getting older
is getting off

more than ever

even though
you have

cellulite

❈❈

On a collision course
with the dark side
of forty

I can only say

I know enough
not to mind
that the law of
gravity
is true

The sex is better
than ever

So why
should
I worry?

Forty-two is
old!
Forty-two is going to your

twentieth college reunion
& lamb stew
& crashing breasts
& confidence
& puckered thighs
& champagne
& condos
& caviar
& laughter
& compromise
& really good sex
& pasta
& wine
& fear
& growing up

MIDDLE-AGED THANKSGIVING

a rarified
menu

(low fat)

won't help keep death away

for long

so screw it

put those

bits o' brickle

on the apple pie

at first I thought
they were freckles
they're liver spots
I suppose I shouldn't
be
surprised

(After all
my liver
has been through a lot
& a lot
has been through
my liver)

But still
I am

❋ ❋

I found out
today
that I
must learn
to live
with chronic pain
all the people
who
I considered
pains in the
neck
Have come back
to haunt me
(literally)
I just want to say
that after many
eons of
costly psychotherapy
my masochistic
tendencies
are well under
control
& now . . .
this happens—
I have chronic pain
& I don't get off
on it at all

Why does masochism
go away
just when you
get old
& need it most?

TIME

The sun & the
                moon

                play musical chairs

in very slow motion

How did I get to be

                50?

IMPERMANENCE
(ain't it the truth)

Frank had a
massive coronary

& Kay has
ovarian cancer
(mets) to the
bones

& I,
even I,
have way fewer

teeth
& uteruses
than I could have
& you have
low thyroid
& high cholesterol
&
an enlarged prostate
& we had
some really good
sex
last night
for a couple of old coots
or young ones

THERE IS SOMETHING

There is something
        like how the—I don't know—odor
of burning leaves
can suck you back
to being five in the country in August
and you Are
'til your mind
pokes it and
it's gone
That sort of something

Have we met before?
        please
I can't quite place
                your face   though
there is something . . .

was it on a boat ride
'round Manhattan
in summer dusk
when skies turned buildings
from pink to gray
and buildings, water, wind and me
were one
setting slowly
with the sun?

but no
that day
has many years
been done
still   there is something so . . .

I'm 54

& life
as I have always
known it

may not be
what I thought

when I let go

there is all this stuff
& nothing
at the same time

Thank God it
doesn't happen
very often

❋ ❋

I spent the first
hours
of my 55th birthday

with a
breast man

then I went
to the
Doctor
who was also
a breast man
so he could
check out
a small lump
in my right
breast

I've been
felt up
(as we say)
by some
real pros
But this guy
had
gold
in the fingers
& said,
"Well, it feels perfectly
normal to me
a little lumpy
But you're fine"

Happy Birthday!

I think my thighs
are better now (in front)
than when I was
twenty-five

I can't be sure, though

Because I never really
looked at them
when I was
twenty-five

❋ ❋

Getting older

is knowing
you have
a small talent
for writing
poems
and seeing this
as reason
to rejoice
rather than pout

is seeing
that
being sane
makes me
more anxious
than neurosis
ever dreamed

❋ ❋

HAPPY BIRTHDAY—NOT

When I was fifty
I thought it was nifty
& fifty-one
was lots of fun
and fifty-two
fit
just like a shoe
& fifty three
is where I want to be

because
54 seems so *much* more
so at 53 I'll stay
& tomorrow will be
just another day

The best thing
about being
an alcoholic
            is

You can always
find something
to celebrate
            with a drink
the worst thing
            is,
                        you

can always find
something to be
anxious or depressed
            about
for which
            you need
a drink

Also, the mornings suck
                        either way

Some really good thighs are born—
most Jewish thighs are not

❈ ❈

OK

I wouldn't
MIND
a cigarette
right now
or
whenever

OK—now is good,

But
someone disguising
herself
as me
apparently
quit
smoking
& gave my name
it must be
some mistake

❈ ❈

I don't have

anorexia

or bulimia

But I did have

a root canal

2 days before

Thanksgiving

not that I had
a lot of choice
But still

Thanksgiving Root Canal

must be
a very
esoteric
Axis I eating disorder NOS
(not otherwise
specified)

❋❋

It happens to all of us

the best of us
& the worst of us
Everyone that you
know & love
or don't even like
that much

Dies

unless you're lucky
enough
or unlucky enough
to die first

48

Even our dogs

are turning gray

My dad always said . . .

"When you mature
things are no longer
black or white

but gray"

He was right

first they're gray
then
they fade away
altogether
or turn blonde
I never thought I'd go blonde
I never thought
I'd die
I was wrong goodbye

The only good thing
about

a root canal
is

it sounds
as bad
as it is

they say
"You need a
root
canal"

& you say,

oh shit.

❈ ❈

imagine
        if someone

put a jack hammer
        in your mouth

& commenced jack hammering?

well,
        multiply that
                times infinity,

and that's what

        a root canal
                feels like,
if you're very lucky

        (& not Jewish)

It's 3 a.m.
        & I am
experiencing some of that possible discomfort
you hear about
        following a root canal
earlier today

It's not surprising
        really
if you think about
        just the words
                Root Canal
somehow contain
        enormous pain
a canal should
        join 2 waterways
not occur inside
                a tooth

Before I had
my gums
removed

the periodontist
said:

"You may experience
a little discomfort"
(my personal favorite example of Doctor speak)
and

"Don't worry

Your insurance
will cover
everything"

Well you guessed it
I did

& it didn't

& Doctor
my check
is in
the mail

Lost some teeth
    Lost my Dog
Lost my uterus
    Lost my ovaries
Lost my bone mass

    Lost my brain cells
Lost my lung capacity
    Lost my elasticity

Kept my breasts
    (so far
    for now)

Thank you God,

for leaving me

a few bottom teeth

with which

to build a bridge

to the 21st century

I can't help

wishing
you could have
seen your way

to do the same
on top

⁂

So
    you worked very hard
        & eventually

you became

    a dentist

But even that

was not enough

to satisfy

    your secret

        sadistic longings

so

    Endodontistry

was right up

    your alley—

❋ ❋

I was brushing
        my (8) remaining
teeth, before
my dental appointment,
when it
        occurred
that to me
"too little
        &
too late"
could be
        the age old
adage I
have lived by,
which
        worked well
when I was young
but,
        as it becomes
too late
        no longer
seems to be
        the way
                to go

I really knew

I was old

when it was time
to get all my
upper teeth pulled

& my dentist
was too senile
to do it

❋❋

My mind
needs
a haircut

my liver
needs
a transplant

my mornings
need to
begin
at noon

maybe
I need
to stop
drinking

❋❋

It's coming
    up
on 2 weeks
& thanks to
several
    nicotine
products
    used
    simultaneously
(despite
    warnings
to the
contrary)
& all I can say
    is
I would really
like a cigarette
very soon

    NOW
would be
    good

Well
I've quit smoking
after 44 years of not
(or I haven't had a
cigarette for 9 weeks
which is close enough)
& now,
I would be well-advised
to quit drinking alcohol
smoking marijuana & taking
medicine to temper
   my pain
I really think
   it's a lot
      to expect
from an aging
   junky
let's just say
   I know the direction
   in which to go
& I'm giving it   a reasonable
      shot
but I don't
   believe
in MIRACLES

I haven't seen that many
   only you

ADDICTION

OK,
imagine this:
You're a girl
& you have
an uncle
who is 6'5"
& looks better
than Rock Hudson
(before we knew about Rock Hudson)
& now (this uncle) he's 73
& weighs
140 lbs.
because
he has lung cancer
& you
still smoke
& your father
died of emphysema
& you love your mate
& your work & your family
& your friends, & your dogs
& you
are
still smoking

The hardest thing
for a junkie
to learn
(almost—no actually—by definition)
is moderation.
AA says it can't be done

they may be right

But I here highly

resolve

To give it
my best shot

& if I do

I'll take half the credit
my "enabler," my lover,
my friend, gets the rest
& the higher power
don't get shit

❋❋

Sun is bad
Yet tan is good

I've never known
Quite where I stood

Sun rays feel so warm & swell
But I just burn
& get Basal Cell

❋❋

I was talking today
to a woman
who is sure she has
Alzheimer's disease
& she said:
I can't imagine
what my life will be like
& I said:
me neither
& I don't even have it
Your problem isn't
Alzheimer's disease
whether you have it
or not
It's thinking you should be
able to imagine
what your life
will be like

❈❈

GETTING OLDER

Youth
is worse than
arthritis.

Beauty
transformed
into
wisdom.

Seems like
a reasonable deal.

❈❈

ANOTHER GETTING OLDER POEM

Yesterday
my husband bought
2 Porterhouse steaks
&
we only cooked one

it was enough

& then

we didn't want

strawberry shortcake

for dessert

& we weren't

even

on a diet

Youth:

oh, shit

Middle age:

oh, shit
oh, well

Old age:

oh well